Anonymous

Authentic Abstracts of Minutes in the Supreme Council of Bengal

Anonymous

Authentic Abstracts of Minutes in the Supreme Council of Bengal

ISBN/EAN: 9783743401655

Manufactured in Europe, USA, Canada, Australia, Japa

Cover: Foto ©Suzi / pixelio.de

Manufactured and distributed by brebook publishing software
(www.brebook.com)

Anonymous

Authentic Abstracts of Minutes in the Supreme Council of Bengal

AUTHENTIC

ABSTRACTS

O F

MINUTES

IN THE

SUPREME COUNCIL

O F

BENGAL,

On the late Contracts for Draught and Carriage Bullocks, for victualling the European Troops, and for victualling Fort William; the Augmentation of General Sir Eyre Coote's Appointment, and Continuation of Brigadier-General Stibbert's Emoluments, though superseded in the Chief Command; and a remarkable Treaty, offensive and defensive, with the Ranah of Gohud, a Marratta.

———————

LONDON:

Printed for J. Almon opposite Burlington-House, Piccadilly.
MDCCLXXX.

P R E F A C E.

AT a time that the Britiſh empire is over-
whelmed with taxes and debt, that the
ravages of war are depopulating the realm, that
the colonies and ſettlements abroad (which were
the ſinews of its wealth and ſuperiority) are diſ-
membering from it, and that unnatural diſcon-
tents and feuds at home, are ſapping and diſ-
uniting its internal reſources and power; it becomes the duty of individuals, by the expoſure
of authentic facts, to exhibit before the Mini-
niſters of Government, and the Public, the fatal
errors which have led to ſome of thoſe unhappy
embarraſsments; and to rouſe them to a ſenſe
of what they owe to their ſtations, and to them-
ſelves, as the means of ſaving a remnant, upon
which to raiſe a ſuperſtructure, ſuperior even
to what it has been.

The abuſes committed in the Supreme Council of Bengal are ſo voluminous, that it would

a be

be almoft impoffible (however interefting the
fubject) to exhibit them to the public, fo as to
fecure due attention to them, in any other fhape,
than by piece-meal.

The *contracts* which Mr. Haftings and Mr.
Barwell carried into execution, by Mr. Haftings's *cafting vote*, as Governor-General, againft
the remonftrances and votes of Mr. Francis and
Mr. Wheler in the latter end of 1779; the advance, falaries, and emoluments voted to General
Sir Eyre Coote, as Commander in Chief; and
the continuation of a Commander in Chief's appointment to Brigadier-General Stibbert *after* he
was fuperfeded, have been topics of converfation
in Britain; but the partial difplay of mifreprefen-
tation *defignedly*, hath impofed upon the credulity
of many. As thefe compofe a part of the evils
which threaten the fpeedy extinction of the Eaft-
India Company, and fubverfion of the Britifh
commerce and poffeffions in India, they are made
the fubject of the following fheets, at a time
that Minifters are again obliged to bring the affairs of the Company before Parliament. A
Treaty of a curious nature and complexion with
the diftreffed and reduced Ranah of Gohud is
annexed, as well to fhew the real principles of

action,

action, as the unaccountable infatuation which have guided the political faculties of men, cried up in this country, as prodigies for superior talents. Other facts are to follow forthwith, amongst which the origin and history of the present Marratta war, the late war whereby the Company's troops, *as mercenaries,* exterminated the Robilla nation, and the present actual situation and disposition of the several states and powers in Hindoftan, combined and closely leagued into a strict confederacy against the English, on principles of self-preservation.

In March 1777, there were above £.1,500,000 sterling unappropriated in the treasuries of Bengal. In August 1778, Mr. Hastings and Mr. Barwell pledged themselves, that after making liberal allowances for all extra contingencies, there would remain unappropriated in the Treasury, on the 31st of March following, £.2,056,000; yet at the prefixed period, there was not £.10,000 unappropriated. And by a positive resolution which originated under Mr. Hastings's pen in the month of November 1778, the Company's investments were in future reduced

duced from 140 *to* 100 *lacks of rupees. The last estimate of probable resources and actual disbursements, from March* 1780 *to April* 1781, *unanimously authenticated by every Member of the Council Board, and transmitted to the Court of Directors, discovered a real deficiency of near £.300,000, after accounting for, and appropriating the deposit of £.359,000, in Fort William. The Treasury of Oude, which paid a subsidy of about £.950,000 a year to the Company, was exhausted, and the Company's troops in the provinces dependent upon the Nabob, were in arrears, some six, and none less than three months. Native troops in India are like the Swiss troops in Europe; the stoppage of pay is the stoppage of service; mutiny and desertion are the certain consequence; and the troops regularly trained and disciplined by the Company, will augment the armies of their enemies. What the event will be, needs no prophetic faculty, unless measures, as well as men, are changed.*

MINUTES

MINUTES

IN THE

SUPREME COUNCIL

OF

BENGAL

ON THE

BULLOCK CONTRACT.

August 31ſt, 1779.

Minute from Mr. *Francis* and Mr. *Wheeler*.

WE have great reaſon to complain of the uncom‑
mon hurry and precipitation, with which the
propoſed contract for ſupplying the army with draught
and carriage bullocks for five years, has been engroſſed
and brought before the board to be executed on Thurſ‑
day the 26th inſtant. Conſidering the very extraordi‑
nary charge which the Company is to incur by this con‑
tract, and the number of new and intricate clauſes and
proviſions of which it conſiſts, it was the ſecretary's
duty to have prepared a draft of the contract, and to
have ſubmitted it to the approbation of the board, be‑
fore he gave directions to the attorney for having it en‑
groſſed. This neceſſary form not having been obſerved,

B   we we have not a sufficient time allowed us to consider every article of the contract, with the attention it deserves; but this shall not prevent our laying before the board such remarks as immediately occur to us, in hopes that they may still be early enough to induce the other members to weigh the subject more deliberately, and not to put their names to an instrument, in which, as we think, the Company's interest is entirely sacrificed, and their orders flatly disobeyed. If, nevertheless, a majority of the board should persist in their intentions to execute the contract, we shall have done as much as depends upon us at present, by stating our objections to it, and, shewing the consequences that must attend it, supposing the contract to take effect.

We have already referred to the Company's instructions relative to contracts in general; but as we find that in the year 1770, the court of directors had entered into a very minute enquiry, concerning the particular contract for furnishing draught and carriage bullocks, we beg leave to annex a copy of the order they gave at that time, from which we shall only quote the following words in this place, that the members of the board who have it in contemplation to give away the contract for five years, may know at the same time, that they are setting the Company's authority at defiance:

" It is our express order, and we hereby positively direct, that you do not fail every year, to advertise for, and receive such proposals, as may be offered for supplying the troops with provisions, and for furnishing draught and carriage bullocks to be employed with our army. And that you do in all cases accept those proposals, which may appear the most reasonable in point of charge."

The annexed paper No. 2, contains a comparison of the expence of the present establishment of bullocks, supposing suppofing it compleat according to the contract now exifting, with that which is to be cre ted by the propofed contract. By this it appears 'that the former 'is Sicca rupees 13,786 : 3 anas per month, and the latter Sicca rupees 58,629 making the enormous difference or increafe of Sicca rupees 44,842 : 13 anas per month. On this footing the bullock contract will coft. the Company, no lefs than current rupees 8,16,120 per annum, for five years certain, or current rupees 40,80,600. (408,060l. fterling) And this exceffive charge cannot, according to the terms of the contract, be reduced a fingle rupee during the five years; at the fame time that openings are defignedly left to increafe it confiderably.

We folemnly proteft again{t every attempt to load the Company with fuch an immoderate expence, and particularly againft the intention, to fix it irrevocably for any term of years. In the contract now exifting, and in all the former bullock contracts, a claufe has been invariably inferted, by which the Company or the Government here, or even the Colonels of the brigade, had a power referved to them of difcharging any number of fuperfluous, or unneceffary bullocks, giving one month's notice to the contractor; but no fuch claufe is inferted in the intended contract, fo that the Company muft at all events, keep up the entire number of 6700 bullocks for five years, or at leaft pay for them, under every change of circumftances whatfoever, and even though they fhould find it neceffary to reduce or new model their army in the mean time.

In the propofed contract no diftinction is made between draught and carriage bullocks, or whether within or without the provinces. Every bullock is to be paid for at the rate of Sicca rupees, 8 : 12 anas, per month,
R. A. P.
or Sonat rupees, 9. 2. 3 ½, including the divers.

By

By the prefent contract without the provinces, a
draught bullock employed or unemployed   R. A. P.
is Sonat rupees   —   —   5 : 0 : 0
Carriage ditto   —   —   3 : 10 : 0
Draught and carriage unemployed within the
     provinces   —   —   —   2 : 9 : 6
And for this he feeds them, and finds them in divers,
pads, ropes, &c.

The difference between the two rates is fo extraordinary, that we imagine no member of the board, who
gives his attention to the fubject, will ever confent to it.

In the third article of the propofals, it is ftated that
condemned bullocks fhall be thrown on the hands of the
contractor, but without any penalty, which we think
there ought to be, confidering how much the fervice
may fuffer; and that he is allowed 12 Sicca rupees per
annum, for every bullock in the army, to make good
loffes that may happen by the enemy, death, *rejection*, &c.
befides a bounty of 10 Sicca rupees, for every extra bullock found, upon notice given.

He is to incur a penalty of three times the actual Bazar
price of the gram, if the bullocks are not victualled a-
greeably to the terms of the contract. The latter part,
the commanding officer of the brigade, and commanding officer of the artillery may certify on the bills; but
as the commiffary-general is to be the check, how is he
to know the *actual bazar price* of gram at the feveral fta-
tions? We think it would be much better to have the
penalty fixed at a certain rate.

By the fifth article the contractor is to be paid by
extra bills, for any increafe of food given to the bullocks, by orders of the commanding officer. This we
think highly unreafonable, as the terms of the contractor

tor are in themfelves already much too liberal, and it
is the intereft of the contractor, that his bullocks fhould
be properly fed.

The expence of drivers, firdars-drivers, bridles, picket
ropes, pads, &c. was never before charged to the Company.

Loffes by forced marches, or over loading, are to be
made good to the contractor. He is allowed a Sicca
rupee per month for each bullock, to make good loffes
by the enemy, death, rejection, &c. Every bullock
that dies, will be drawn for, on either of thofe accounts.
It is difficult to afcertain the fact, but if the claufe is admitted, at what rate is the commiffary-general to allow,
within and without the provinces for draught, and for
carriage bullocks which have died, owing to thofe two
caufes; and what proof or evidence is he to accept, that
the death of the bullock was owing to one or other of
the above caufes?

Is it meant that the bullocks loaded with grain for
feeding the other bullocks, are to be at the expence of
the Company? If not there was no occafion for the
fourteenth article, as they always have been, and muft
be allowed to attend the army.

The bounty of ten Sicca rupees for every extra bullock found in a certain time, as expreffed in the fifteenth
article, is unneceffary, at leaft the fum propofed is a
great deal too much. By the prefent contract nothing
is allowed for the purchafe of bullocks, unlefs required
within a month's notice; and if, on fuch emergency, the
ufual price of bullocks fhould be thereby enhanced, he
is allowed for any extra price, that may have been ac-

R. A.

tually paid more than Sonat rupees, 12. 8. for each
draught

-draught bullock, and 8 Sonat rupees for each carriage bullock, but if he does not pay more than those prices, he is to be allowed nothing.

In the bounty there is no diftinction made, betwixt extra draught, and extra carriage bullocks. The former ought furely to coft more than the latter, at leaft there has been always a difference, both in the price, and charges of feeding, hitherto. Confidering the time al-lowed in the fifteenth article, no bounty fhould be given; the contractor is fufficiently rewarded by the increafe, without any other emolument.

If the bills are not prefented by the contractor's agent to the officers, whofe duty it is to counterfign them, with-in a certain number of days after the mufter, the con-tractor fhould be liable to a deduction of 10 per cent. Many irregularities are produced, from bills being drawn fometimes ten and twelve months in arrears. After the words, " that the bills fhould not lay above eight days in the commiffary-general's office," it fhould be added, " unlefs he has occafion to make reference to the officers who have counterfigned the bills," as this will neceffarily occafion fome delay.

In order to enable the contractor to execute this moft lucrative contract, he is to have the value of three-fourths of his ftock, advanced to him out of the treafuries when he may require it: and by the following article, we are to provide him with a piece of ground for keeping his cattle. As we know not in what terms, to exprefs our difapprobation of thefe extravagant conditions, we fhall content ourfeives with ftating them for the Company's obfervation.

The penalty of 50 Sicca rupees for every bullock, hired from officers civil or military, feems to us a nuga-
tory

tory claufe, thrown out for no other purpofe but to give the contract an air of rigour, which by no means belongs to it. Such a penalty can never be enforced.

To conclude, we fuggeft thefe curfory remarks to the board, as fatal to the propofed contract on its own principles, and exclufive of the legality of granting a contract on any conditions for the term in queftion. Many other objections we doubt not would occur to perfons better verfed in the fubject than we are; but what has been faid we truft will be fufficient to juftify to the Company and to the public in general, the part we have taken, or may hereafter take in refifting fo enormous and unprecedented a wafte of the Company's property.

(Signed)   P. FRANCIS.
               E. WHELER.

No. II.

COMPARISON between the expence of the prefent and propofed BULLOCK CONTRACT.

Propofed Contract.

4000 Draught 2700 Carriage	Bullocks at 5. 12.	38,525
A driver to every two bullocks is 3,350 at 5.		16,750
A firdar driver to every fix pair of bullocks is 559. firdar driver at 6.		3,354
Total monthly expences of the propofed contract		58,629

PRESENT

PRESENT CONTRACT TERMS and number of bullocks with the army, fuppofing the fame number with the temporary as with the 1ft brigade in the field, agreeable to the eftablifhment.

640 draught bullocks with the 1ft brig. in the field.
640 ditto ditto, with the temporary brigade.

		R.	A.
1280	draught bullocks, at 5 rupees —	6,400 :	—

1125 ditto with the two brigades at the Prefidency and Burrampore
36 ditto with the light infantry

		R.	A.
1161	draught bullocks, at 3. 7.	3,990 :	15

306 carriage bullocks with the 1ft brigade.
306 ditto ditto with the temporary brigade.

		R.	A.
612	carriage bullocks, at 3. 10.	2,218 :	8

550 ditto with the two brigades at the Prefidency and Burrampore.
14 ditto with the light infantry.

		R.	A.
564	carriage bullocks, at 3. 3.	1,797 :	12

Total monthly expence of the bullocks for the army, by the prefent contract, fuppofing the eftablifhment complete.
Sonat Rupees. 14,407 : 3

Monthly expence of the bullocks for the army, by the propofed contract.
Sicca Rupees. 58,629 : —

Monthly

Monthly expence of the bullocks for the army, by the prefent contract.
Sonat Rupees   14,407. 3.   or   13,786 : 3

Difference of expence betwixt the prefent and propofed contract, monthly.   *Sicca Rupees.*   44,842 : 13

Total expence of the propofed contract per annum, according to the fixed eftablifhment, and exclufive of all additional allowances provided for in the faid contract,

	R.	A.	P.
Current rupees	8,16,115 :	10 :	11

	Ct. Rs.	A.	P.
Ditto for five years —	40,80,578 :	6 :	7

BOARD of INSPECTION.

9th September, 1779.

Mr. FRANCIS,

IN addition to the remarks contained in Mr. Wheler's minute and mine of the 31ft of Auguft on the propofed bullock contract, I beg leave to lay the annexed papers before the board, and to requeft the attention of the members to the calculations contained therein, before any farther fteps are taken in this bufinefs. Calculations of this nature ought to have accompanied the plan in the firft inftance, that the board might know what they were doing, and not be hurried blindly into engagements, extent, confequences, and expence, of which they could not poffibly have formed an idea.

C   The

The annexed papers, number 1 and 2, fhew the full amount of all the draught and carriage bullocks neceffary for the compleat fervice of the three entire brigades, fuppofing them all in the field; by which it appears, that the number of bullocks, propofed to be kept up for five years, exceeds what the whole army, on a compleat war eftablifhment, would require, by 2769. Thefe fupernumerary bullocks, therefore, if they are maintained, will have nothing to do. There are not guns or carriages for them to draw. There is literally nothing for them to carry. But before this time, who ever heard of keeping up a compleat war eftablifhment of bullocks, without actual fervice in any part of the provinces. What are the bullocks to do at the prefidency? What are they to do at the different cantonments? In truth I might with great reafon afk (with the exception of a very moderate number) what occafion have we for an eftablifhment of bullocks any where? When they are wanted, they may be hired, or prefs'd, as in fact they have been hitherto, notwithftanding the contract; but admitting that fome eftablifhment ought to be maintained, it will be difficult to affign a good reafon why it fhould exceed the complement neceffary for the troops in the field; fuppofing a third of the army to be maintained on a war eftablifhment, the number of draught and carriage bullocks, taken together, ought not to exceed 1,310.

On this principle, which of itfelf would lead us into an exorbitant expence, the propofed contract is to maintain 5390 bullocks more than can be wanted, which, for five years, at the new contract rates, will be found to amount to the enormous fum of current rupees 32,82,510, abfolutely given away out of the Company's treafury, or fquandered without any neceffity or fervice whatfoever.

No,

No. III.

Contains a calculation of the difference of expence between the propofed eftablifhment, and that which would be neceffary for the whole army in the field, calculated at the new contract rates. Even on this extravagant principle, the expence would fall fhort of the propofed contract by feventeen lacks of current rupees in five years.

No. IV.

Shews what the expence of a compleat eftablifhment for the whole army would amount to, if calculated at the *prefent* contract rates. The difference between this and the propofed rates and numbers, amounts in five years to no lefs than current rupees, 30,48,854, or very near three hundred and five thoufand pounds fterling.

If a majority of the Board, with fuch glaring facts before them, can entertain a thought of proceeding farther in the propofed contract, I cannot hope that they will pay the leaft regard to any obfervations I can make upon it. To acquit myfelf, neverthelefs, of the duty I owe to the Company on this important occafion, I think it right to ftate the following general obfervations. My prefent ill ftate of health will not allow me to go fo deep into the fubject, as I fhould do at another time.

Although no evil is more feverely felt, yet there is not apparently any lefs attended to than the number of followers of the army: they confift of a multitude of predatory vagrants, and whatever tends to encreafe their numbers, tends to embarrafs and impede the fervice.

Provifions

Provisions and forage are not only rendered *constantly* dearer than they need be, but frequent scarcities of both are occasioned by this rabble, which thereby bring into imminent danger the safety and existence of the troops.

In this view the number of bullock drivers proposed, appears to be highly detrimental to the good of the service. It would not be credited in Europe, that 12 bullocks should require seven keepers. But this is not the extent of the evil; some, at least, of those seven, will carry with them their families. Those have their attendants with bullocks, or tattoes*, to carry their provisions; and those must have drivers, who also must have provisions. Thus the number of followers encreases beyond calculation; measures tending to reduce their numbers would be useful indeed, and deserving of the highest applause. But what shall we say of schemes which manifestly tend to encrease them? What effect can they have, but to encrease the confusion of our camps, to enhance the difficulty of procuring forage and provisions, to extend and weaken the line of march, and, in the end, to make our army little better than a convoy for the baggage.

Having not had it in my power to enter into a particular consideration of the new victualling contract, I take this opportunity of declaring, that I entirely concur in Mr. Wheler's remarks upon it. I find it is formed upon the same exorbitant principles with the bullock contract, and to be executed by the same persons; that is, a variety of concealed interests are to be provided for, under the name of Mr. Crofts. On this part of the subject I must observe, that the two contracts ought not, on any account, to be in the same hands; no one person is equal to the conduct of two such extensive concerns.

In

---

* Tattoes are small hardy horses.

In the second place, I must declare, that the present contractors, whoever they are, are the most improper persons that could be chosen for the like trust in future. The contracts were never so ill executed, as by the present contractors. Their bullocks have never been ready, or fit for service, when called upon ; and the provisions issued to the Europeans, particularly the beef, has been such as must have produced a mortality among them, if they had eaten it.

The contractor has never given an ounce of mutton to the Europ-ans in Fort William since February last; in consequence of which, they have usually taken cowries in lieu of the carrion beef, with which he would have supplied them.

On the increase of the rates in both contracts, there is one general observation to be made, which, I think, must strike every man conversant in public business.

In engaging for the supply of any article whatsoever, the contractor proportions his rate of price to the quantity of the thing demanded. If he supplies a little, his rate, or price, must be proportionably higher. If he supplies a great deal, he can afford to reduce his terms, since the profit upon the whole compensates for the reduction on the rate of each specification. In the proposed bullock contract, this universal principle is manifestly reversed. The number of bullocks, on the pay of which the contractors profit is to arise, is encreased in nearly the proportion of seventeen to nine ; and the period, during which the contract is to endure, is enlarged from one year to five. One would expect from this encrease of the period, and the number, that the rates would have been proportionally diminished. On the contrary, however, the Company will find, that the rated pay of each individual

dual

dual bullock, lumping the draught and carriage bullocks together, is double what it was.

Upon the whole, the terms, voluntarily contrived
and given by Government, are such, as I presume, no
man living would have presumed to have demanded,
if the contract had been advertised in the manner prescribed by the Company's most peremptory and repeated orders.

(Signed)   P. FRANCIS.

No. I.

Proportion of Ordinance for one Brigade, consisting of
one Regiment of Europeans, eleven battalions of
Seapoys, and a detachment of the Corps of Artillery,
shewing the number of draught bullocks necessary
for dragging its train, and for that of the whole
army.

4 twelve pounder brass guns, with carriage, ten bul- locks to each	40
28 six ditto, with ditto, eight ditto	224
4 five and half inch howitzer, six ditto	24
29 tumbrils ammunition loaded, ten ditto	290
1 ditto treasure, ten ditto	10
2 carts, artificers, ten ditto	20
1 waggon for gin, sixteen ditto	16

Spare

Spare Carriage and Tumbrils.

1 for twelve pounders, eight bullocks — 8
7 for six ditto, six ditto — — 42
1 for five and half-inch howitzer, six ditto 6
7 for tumbrils, six ditto . — — 42

722
Allow one spare to every six bullocks   120

Complement of draught bullocks for one ⎱ 842
   brigade on service ⎰ .3

Ditto for three brigades — — 2526
Independant Chittagong battalion — 30
Battalion of light infantry — 30

Total draught bullocks neceffary for the field
  ordnance of the whole army, fuppofing it on
  actual fervice — — 2586

According to the eftablifhment of 1777, the complement of ordnance for a brigade on fervice was 26 pieces. Since that period, 2 twelve poundets, and 2 howitzers, have been added, which, with the 6 guns of the three battalions of the temporary brigade that are to be incorporated into each of the other brigades, makes the prefent proportion 36 pieces.

No. 2.

Calculate of carriage bullocks neceffary for carrying the mufquet ammunition and millitary ftores, attached to a brigade on fervice, fuppofing it to be of the
        ftrength

ftrength fpecified in No. I. fhewing the number neceffary for the whole army, fuppofing it to be in
motion.

196 Carriage bullocks will carry 329 barrels of mufquet ball ammunition, each barrel containing
800 pounds, to · — — 313,600

Suppofing a brigade to confift of 9580
men, and that 8500 of them are fit
for fervice, they will carry in their
pouches, at 24 pounds per man   1,70,000

Total mufquet cartridges for a brigade
on fervice — — · 4,83,600

50 Carriage bullocks will carry 160 lb. barrels of
powder, being the ufual proportion for fervice.

130 Carriage bullocks, and 20 haccaries, which are
not provided by the contractor, it is believed, are
fufficient for the carriage of the other ftores in the
magazine (No. 5.) exclufive of the above haccaries, the captains of battalion and quarter-matters
are allowed 18, and the furgeon major 10 haccaries.

376
63 Spare bullocks in the proportion of one to fix.

439 Total number of carriage bullocks neceffary to be
provided by the contractor for one brigade on
fervice.

878 Add for two other brigades on fervice.

1317

1317 Total carriage bullocks for three brigades.
  14 Allow for the Chittagong independent battalion.
  14 Allow for the battalion of light infanty.
  _____
1345 Grand total carriage of bullocks.

_____

No. 3.

Calculate of the extra expence that would be incurred
  by the number of bullocks and drivers, suppoſing no
  excefs in the rates propofed.

4000 Draught ⎱ Bullocks at 8. 12. or 923. $\frac{7}{11}$ includ-
1345 Carriage ⎰ ing drivers wages as propofed per month,
              Sicca Rupees 58629.
____
6700
____

2586 Draught ⎱ Bullocks neceffary for the ⎱ R.   A.
1345 Carriage ⎰ train of the whole army, at ⎰
              the above rate per month, ⎰34,401 : 4
              Sicca rupees ⎰

     Monthly difference   Sic. Rup. 24227 : 12

     Annual difference ——— ——— 290733 : ———

Difference that would be occafioned in
  five years by mere excefs of bullocks,
  at the rates propofed, Sicca Rupees   R. A. P.
  14,53,665, or current rupees 16,86,251 : 6 : 5

                    D   No.

No. 4.

Comparison between the expence of the proposed contract, and the neceffary number of bullocks for the
whole army at the prefent contract rates, fuppofing half
the troops to be without, and the other half within the
Provinces, and the whole on actual fervice.

Proposed contract eftablifhment, as before ftated, per
month   Sicca rupees 58629

Neceffary Eftablifhment.

1293 Draught bullocks
     without the pro-   6465
     vinces, at 5 rup.

 673 Carriage ditto,   R. A.
      ditto, at   3 10   2439 10

1293 Draught   at 3 7 4444 11
 672 Carriage.   Bullocks in
             provinces
         at 3 3 2142

       Sonat rupees 15491 5 or Sa. 14823 10

    Monthly difference, Sicca rupees   43805 6

          Annual difference   525664 8

   Diff. in 5 yrs. Son. rups. 2628322 8
   or current rupees   —   30,48,854 1 7

Proof of the difference.

Annual expence of the propofed
     contract, Sic. Rups. 7,03,548,
     or Cur. Rups. 8,16,115 10 11
     which for 5 yrs is curt. rups   40,80,578 6 7

                             Annual

Annual expence of the neceſſary
eſtabliſhment, according to the
preſent contract rates, Sicca Rupee, 1,77,883 8, or Current
Rups. 2,06,344 13 9¾. which
for five years is Current Rups. 10,31,724 5
Diff. as above, Current Rups. 30,48,854 1 7

Board of Inſpection, September 1779.

Mr. *Wheler*. In addition to Mr. Francis's accounts,
I beg leave to preſent the accompanying calculate,
No. 5. in order to demonſtrate, that even upon the
extravagant ſuppoſition of the neceſſity of keeping up
a conſtant eſtabliſhment of 6700 bullocks, an exceſs of
expence will ariſe in 5 years from the exorbitant increaſe
of the conſtant rates, of no leſs than Current Rupees
23,44,191 : 8 : 5. being above two hundred and
thirty four thouſand pounds ſterling; and having
eſtabliſhed this fact, which, with what Mr. Francis has
ſaid, ſufficiently expoſes the complexion of this tranſ-
action, and cuts off every poſſible plea of juſtification.
I have at preſent only to add, that I join Mr. Francis
in reprobating the projected contract, as a meaſure
big with the moſt ruinous conſequences to the Company.

(Signed)   E. W.

Calculate of ſurplus expence that would ariſe from the
increaſe of rates, ſuppoſing the whole number of
Draught and Carriage Bullocks ſpecified in the *propoſed* contract to be neceſſary, and one half of that
number to be without, and the other half within
the Provinces.

D 2   4000

4000 Draught ⎫ Bullocks, being the   Sic. Rups.
2700 Carriage ⎬ propofed contract
          ⎭ eftablifhment, as
        fpecified in No. 3.   58629 : —

2000 Draught Bullocks out
     of the provinces, at
     the prefent contract
     rate, 5 Sonat Rupees
 - each, Sont. Rups.   1000

2000 Ditto within the pro-
     vinces, at the pre-
     fent contract rate,
     R. A.
     at 3 : 7 each —   6875

4000 Total draught bul-
     locks propofed per
     month, at the pre-
     fent contract rates,
     Sonat Rupees   16,875

1350 Carriage   bullocks,
     without the pro-
     vinces, at the pre-
     fent contract rate, at
     R. A.   R. A.
     3 : 10 each, 4893 : 12

1350 Ditto within the pro-
     vinces, at the pre-
     fent contract rate, at
     R. A.
     3 : 3 each, 4303 : 2

                             2700

2700 Total carriage bul-
 locks, propofed
 at the prefent
 contract rate, per
 month   9196 : 14

To monthly expence
 of the propofed
 contract eftablifh-
 ment of draught &
 carriage bullocks,
 at the prefent con-
 tract rates, Snt. R. 26,071 : 14, or 24,948 : 1 : 4 $\frac{88}{0}$

Monthly difference between the
 propofed and prefent contract
 rates —— Sic. Rups. 33,680 : 14 : 7 $\frac{28}{118}$

Yearly difference   Sic. Rups. 4,04,170 : 15 : 2 $\frac{104}{110}$

Total extraordinary expence that
 would be occafioned in 5 years,
 by the mere increafe of rates,
 fuppofing no excefs in the number of bullocks propofed, Sicca
 Rupees, 20,20,854 : 12 : 2, or
 Current Rupees ——   23,44,191 : 8 : 5

Minutes on the Army Victualling Contract.

Read the following letter from the Executor of the
late Army Contractor.

            Infpection

Infpection Board, 19th Auguft, 1779.

Honoured Sir, and Sirs,

I HAVE been honoured through your fecretary *with your proffer of certain alterations in the army bullock contract; I voluntarily accept them*, and having, with a view to the liquidation of my brother's eftate, transferred its concern in this, as well as the victualling contract, to Mr. Charles Croftes, who was before a partner in them, I humbly requeft the new contracts may both be made out in his name, and further hope, that as thefe two contracts have always been kept in the fame hands, that they will now be both granted for the fame term.

Fort-William, 16th   I am, &c.
Auguft, 1779.   (Signed) RICH. JOHNSON.

Agreed that the new contract for fupplying the draught and carriage cattle; and victualling the troops of this eftablifhment, be drawn in the name of Mr. Charles Croftes, and that the latter contract be extended for the fame term as the former.

Mr. *Francis.* I object to it, and proteft againft it.

Mr. *Wheler.* I have already given my opinion againft the recital of either of thefe contracts for a term not exceeding one year, and fhall not fign them ; neverthelefs, fo far as relates to the inferting of one name inftead of the other, I acquiefce, believing the party to have had a fhare in the former contract.

The Secretary lays before the Board, the following letter from the Executor to the late Army Contractor.

Sir,

Sir,

I HAVE received your letter of this date, and accept the terms it contains.

The contract allows 10 Sonat Rupees full batta, and
5 rupees for half batta, for beef per month, or 5 Anas,
4 Pice, each man per day, full batta, and 2 Anas 8
Pice. per each man per day half batta, for the period
that motion is required, I agree to deliver it for 7
Ana's 6 Pice. each man per day half batta, for the
period that motion is required, I agree to deliver it for
7 Ana's 6 Pice. each man per day, full batta, and 3
Ans. 9 Pice. each man per day, half batta.

Fort William, the   I am, &c.
   18th Aug. 1779.   (Signed) R. JOHNSON.

The Board agree to allow the difference required for
the remainder of the contract, but in the new contract
they will only allow the difference of one Ana and one
Pice. per man full batta, and proportionally for half
batta, as by the custom of the service, though not specified on the present contract, beef and mutton ought
to be distributed to the soldiers in equal quantities.

Mr. *Francis.* I cannot agree in this resolution,
because I am no judge of the prices of provisions,
or whether the terms proposed are reasonable or
not; the way to ascertain the cheapest terms on which
government can be served, is by advertising publickly
for proposals.

Mr. *Wheler.*—I can form no judgment of the propriety of the present request, for want of the proper
calculations, which should accompany a proposal of
this sort from the contractor, and those from the regular department of government necessary to contract
                                                    with

with them. I beg to be favoured with the amount
what one Ana one Pice. per man, per day, intended
to be given in the new contract amounts to by the,
year. I likewise wish to have it ascertained, at the
same time, what proportion mutton, for the six months
mentioned in the contractor's letter, bears to beef in
the six following months, and whether the quantity of
each is to be delivered out equally ; that is, whether
during the six months that mutton is delivered, the
garrison is to receive the same number of pounds weight
in mutton, as in beef the six following months.

Governor General.—I have no objection to the latter
part of the question remaining for consideration, but
for the short remainder of the present contract, I propose that the difference he requires be allowed.

Letter from the late Army Contractor's executor,
to Mr. Baugh.

Sir,
I have received the honor of your letter of the 19th
instant.

Having considered the difference that will be occasioned, by supplying mutton instead of beef, I find
it to be one Ana six Pice. sonat, per man per day. For
the delivery of beef at the presidency, I now receive
five Anas and four Pice. In lieu therefore of the alteration you propose, upon my claim for the delivery
of mutton, I beg leave to offer as a medium for the
whole term of the new contract, that the contractor
deliver at the presidency, mutton for the six hot months,
(April to September inclusive) and during the remaining six months, mutton and beef every other day alternately ; for which he shall be permitted to draw, six

Anas

Anas and 10 Pice. fonat per day, throughout the whole year.. This propofal only to vary under the regulation of full and half Batta, which ever the troops at the prefidency may be entitled to receive.

I have, &c.

(Signed)   R. JOHNSON,
Executor to the late Contractor.

Governor General.—The offer made by the contractor, approaches very nearly to the refolution of the board, the propofitions being fince confiderably varied by my fuggeftion to the contractor, as it appears to me neceffary that the allowance of beef and mutton to the foldiers in the winter months, ought to be in equal quantities. I underftand the price of mutton in Calcutta to be juft double the price of beef, and the rate now propofed will be found on examination, to make up the exact difference between the provifion of beef alone at the former rate, and of beef and mutton in the proportion of three-fourths of the latter, and one-fourth of the former at the common rate propofed.

I therefore agree to it.

(Signed)   WARREN HASTINGS.

Mr. *Wheler.*—Almoft every argument ufed in Mr. Francis and my minute of the 31ft of Auguft, on the bullock contract, applies with equal force to the prefent propofal for victualling the troops. The Court of Directors in the 134th paragraph of their general letter by the Mansfield, dated the 23d of March 1770, fay,

" It is our exprefs order, and we hereby pofitively direct, that you do not fail every year to advertife for, and receeive fuch propofals as may be offered, for fupplying the troops with provifions ; and for furnifhing draught and carriage bullocks, to be employed with
E   our

our army, and that you do in all cafes accept thofe
propofals, which may appear the moft reafonable in
point of charge ; and your are alfo to take care in all
your advertifements, a fufficient time be allowed before
the expiration of the contract, which may then fubfift,
or the time which you may limit for receiving propofals for fuch contract."

Unlefs fuch advertifements are made, and a fair
competition allowed, I do not fee how the board can
judge whether the contractor's propofals are reafonable
or not. It cannot be expected, that the members of
this board can be competent judges of the comparative
prices, between beef and mutton in all parts of this
country, within and without the provinces, where
troops may ferve, or at what rates the contractor may
be able to procure them, allowing for the difference,
between wholefale and retail purchafers.

Such a queftion is more fit to be decided by pro-
feffional men, than by members of this council, if left
to make their offers, according to the orders of the
Court of Directors. Some of them would without
doubt bring the moft reafonable propofals before the
board, of which the nature of the fervice was capable,
and it would then belong to the board to judge which
offer was moft advantageous.

I muft however obferve, that the contractor ftates
the difference that will arife by fupplying mutton inftead of beef, to be one ana fix pice fonat per man per
day, and in confequence of engaging to deliver mutton
for the fix hot months, and mutton and beef alternately
for the remainder of the year; he, in oppofition to his
own principles, requires to be paid the difference between the two articles, throughout the whole year.

I do

I do not believe the price of mutton will exceed that of beef, suppofing the quality to be equal, and each confumed in its proper feafon, but granting that the former fhould exceed the latter, even to the extent ftated by the contractor; under what pretence does he claim the addition of one ana and fix pice per man per day, for the whole year, where he contracts only to change or vary the diet for three quarters of a year.

In other refpects, I muft confider myfelf as left entirely without the neceffary information on this fubject, and can therefore only lay before the Council, for the information of the Court of Directors, an eftimate, fhewing the difference and excefs of expence, between the late contract and the prefent propofal, for victualling the European foldiers ftationed at the Prefidency, together with the further excefs, provided the contract be extended to the fupply of the whole European eftablifhment, both within and without the provinces, which will be confiderably increafed when the eftablifhment is compleated, according to the propofals of the Commander in Chief.

I have already objected to the term, and I now object to the conditions of this contract.

Comparative view of the expence of victualling the European foldiers, ftationed at the Prefidency, betwixt the prefent and the propofed contract.

	St.	R.	A.	P.
Prefent Contract.				
Each man for 12 months, at 5 rupees		60	0	0
Propofed Contract.				
Each man for 365 days at 3 annas 5 pices per day — —		77	15	1

Difference

Difference being an yearly excefs on
the prefent contract for each man,
ftationed at the Prefidency   —   17   15   1

       77   15   1   77   15   1

The medium number of Europeans returned at
the Prefidency for the laft three months, including
thofe attached to the third brigade, to the company
of Artillery brigade at the Prefidency, and at Budge-
Budge; the Invalid body-guard, and the European
women and children, is 1645, which, at 17 rupees
15 anas 1 pice, makes the yearly excefs, on the prefent contract for victualling the Europeans attached
to the Prefidency,   Sonat rupees   29515   12   1

753 Europeans returned upon the me-
      dium of three months, with the fe-
      cond brigade at Burrampore, (but
      no women or children are included
      as they are not returned) on half
      batta.

81 Europeans at Chunar and Baxar on
      ditto.
___

834 Men at 17 rupees 15 anas 1 pice, the
      yearly excefs for victualling one man,
      Sonat rupees   —   —   14964   3   6

197 Men returned on an average of three
      months, with the temporary brigade
      on full batta.

871 Men returned on an average of three
      months, with the firft brigade on full
      batta

                         1068 Men

1068 Men at 35 rupees 14 anas 2 pices,
the yearly exception on the prefent
contract for victualling one man,
when on full batta   —   38325 10

Total excefs on the prefent contract for
victualling the Europeans of the army, if
the propofed contract be extended to the
whole European eftablifhment, Sonat rupees, per *annum*   —   82805 9 7

Mr. Barwell and *Sir Eyre Coote* fubfcribe to the opinion of the Governor General.

Refolved, That the propofals of the executor of the
late army contractor, viz, to fupply mutton inftead of
beef, for the provifion of the troops ferving at the
Prefidency, from April to September inclufive; and
during the remaining fix months, mutton and beef
every other day, alternately, for which he fhall be allowed fix anas ten pice fonat per man per day, throughout the whole year, only to vary under the regulation
of full and half batta, which ever the troops at the
Prefidency may be entitled to receive—be agreed to.

Minutes on the contract for victualling Fort William.

Extract proceedings Military Department 9th Auguft,
1779.

Extract minute by the Commander in Chief on the
general eftablifhment and regulations of the army,
under the Prefidency of Fort William, dated 7th
July, 1779.

Sir Eyre Coote.

I approve of the department of provisions and regulations respecting its being kept up.

Governor General.

Having received frequent remonstrances from the agent for this deposit concerning the heavy losses and inconveniences, to which he is subjected by the present indefinite term of his agency, which obliges him to purchase the different articles of the stores at the current prices of the markets, and in such quantities as are specified in the prescribed lists, which, in times of scarcity, can neither be procured of equal qualities, as in seasons of plenty, nor without an increase in the price, sometimes even greatly exceeding the rates prescribed in the table formed by the board. *The Governor General recommends that the agency be converted into a contract, and be fixed for the term of five years.*—The Governor General desires his motion to be inserted in this place, but to prevent any delay in passing the resolutions required, by the subjects expressly submitted to the board by the Commander in Chief, he desires that the opinion of the Board may be received upon it in circulation.

15th August.

Sir Eyre Coote,

I entirely concur in the motion of the Governor-General, *as I am clear that a contractor can act cheaper, and, of course perform the service better, by having his contract for a series of years than for one only, when his profit must be immense even to bear him harmless and much more to secure him a profit, and this is better known than I do, by members of this board, to be the general practice of Europe.*

However, had I not these fundamental principles to induce me to support the Governor General's motion, I should still most heartily join in it from the long knowledge I have of
the

*the merits of Mr. Belli, whose abilities, honour, and integrity
I know to be equal to any charge that Government can confer
upon him,* and which I am confident he will execute with
as much advantage to his employers, as credit to himself,
and those who place him in it.

(Signed) E. COOTE.

Mr. Wheler,

As I have upon a very recent occasion assigned my
reasons for preferring annual contracts to engagements
of a longer period, and as I have likewise endeavoured
to prove that no other can be entered into without sub-
jecting on the one hand, the contractor to an unreason-
able degree of risque, or the Company, on the other,
to an improvident bargain, it remains only for me to
add, that in my opinion, if pains were taken to select
from among the variety of contracts that already have,
or probably very soon will, become the subject of public discussion, it might prove difficult to take from the
mass, one where the fitness of an annual contract in pre-
ference to a longer period was more striking, and where
the arguments in favour of a contrary opinion, can with
less effect or reason be applied.

The advantage and utility of annual contracts, are so
well known in England, that I do not recollect a single
instance among the Company's engagements, whether
for military or naval stores, for provisions, or for any
article either for export or home consumption, where
the contracts or engagements have not expired within
the year; and although I seem called upon by the Commander in Chief to evince the contrary practice, I must
here declare, that those which I had the honour to be
engaged in with government, were for no longer a period.

I may likewise further add, that the public received
no small advantage from the short duration of those contracts,

tracts, yet fufficient encouragement was given to the contractors.

If then the fundamental principles of contracts are as I have ftated them in favour of annual ones, or if the precaution is neceffary, and generally adopted, in a country where the value of each article can be afcertained with fo much facility and eafe, and where either a rife or fall of the markets rarely exceeds five per cent. how much more expedient muft a fimilar regulation prove in Bengal, where there is frequently a fluctuation of thirty per cent.

To prove the utility of entering into engagements for fo long a period as five years, it is neceffary, in my opinion, to ftate very different arguments from thofe made ufe of in the Governor General's minute, viz. It ought to be clearly afcertained that the articles to be contracted for, are fubject to little or no fluctuation, and that they will certainly be procured at or about the fame price, which regulates the markets at the commencement of the contract: without fome fuch rule the contracting parties will become equally expofed to the ill confequences of long engagements, which fhorter ones are better calculated to relieve, if not entirely exempt them from.

In addition to the above arguments it may be neceffary to obferve that a depofit of provifions in Fort William can only be required in the cafe of a war, or the apprehenfion of a war, and that many circumftances may happen which might render it quite unneceffary and leave the contract if extended to the time propofed, an ufelefs burden and expence on the Company.

For

' For thefe reafons I am againft entering into any contract for a term exceeding one year.
(Signed)   E. WHELER.

Mr. Francis.

EVERY objection urged againft difpofing of the
bullock contract for five years in the manner propofed, in my opinion lies with greater force againft
the propofition. Both of them ftand in direct contradiction to the 36th article of the Company's inftructions
to the board, in which it is ordered, " that all contracts with the conditions, be publicly advertifed, and
fealed propofals received for the fame."

The bufinefs of fupplying the fort with ftores, has
hitherto been performed by agency, and this mode
was exprefsly chofen by the Governor General himfelf,
becaufe " *an advertifement for a contract for fuch ftores
would be improper. It would be to tell the world what
provifion was made for the defence of the garrifon.*"

The Governor General now reprefents, that " *he has
received frequent remonftrances from the agent of this department, concerning the heavy loffes and inconveniencies to which
he is fubjected, by the prefent indefinite term of his agency,*"
and on this ground recommends, " *that it be converted
into a contract, and be fixed for the term of five years.*".

It is natural enough that the agent, after enjoying the
moft profitable employment, that I believe ever exifted
under this government, fince January 1777, without
any public complaint of thofe heavy loffes, and inconveniencies, againft which he now remonftrates, fhould
wifh to have it fecured to him for five years longer.—
It is alfo very natural, that at the approaching expiration

F   of

of the government, he fhould feel fome apprehenfion
for the fate of his agency under a new one, and that he
fhould ufe his intereft with a majority of the board; if
poffible to put it out of their fucceffors power to reduce
his immoderate profits, or to make any new arrangement
for the public fervice, in this important department.—
But when he affirms that he has fuffered heavy loffes
and inconveniencies, by the indefinite term of his agency,
fo extraordinary a propofition ought to have been accompanied with fomething like a proof. Nothing lefs
than its being brought before us by the principal member
of the board, could induce me to give it a ferious confideration.

In oppofition to it, I fhall ftate fome facts, which I
believe will fet the matter in a clear light.

1ft. The amount of the provifions fupplied by the
agent fince the commencement of his agency, is current
rupees 370,252 prime coft, as per account annexed.—
This fum is advanced to him by government, as faft as
his fupplies are purchafed, confequently he has not
been fubject to any diftrefs or difficulty to raife money.

He lofes nothing on the head of intereft, and if he is
not very carelefs, or unfkilful in his management, he
ought to have been a confiderable gainer on the original
purchafe of the feveral articles, independent of the profits he may make, by the occafional converfion of the
ftores at favourable opportunities. He has the favour
and protection of government, to fupport him in his
purchafes, which, in this country, is no fmall advantage. He buys great quantities at a time, at what feafon
he pleafes, and is paid at the average rate fixed by the
bazar price of fmall quantities, that is, he buys in grofs,
and in effect fells in retail, and laftly, he trades with a
ftock purchafed for him, with the public money.

2d.

7d. To fecure the agent, however, againft all poffible
loffes, to enable him to keep a conftant ftock, and to
reward him for his trouble, it was originally agreed to
take the opinion of three of the moft repu able merchants
in Calcutta, what might be a reafonable commiffion
on the value of the fupplies, to anfwer all the above
purpofes; and Meff. Robinfon, Killican, and Croftes,
who were confulted on the occafion, reported, that
twenty per cent. per annum, would be a reafonable
commiffion. It was refolved neverthelefs by the Governor-general and Mr. Barwell, againft General Clavering's opinion and mine, that thirty per cent. per annum, fhould be allowed.

3d. The commiffion already drawn by the agent, on
a fupply of current rupees, 370,252 amounts to current
rupees 229,912, that is fince the 10th of March 1777.
His annual commiffion on the above fum, amounts to
current rupees 111,075, yet he complains that he fuffers
heavy loffes and inconveniencies, by the indefinite term of
his agency.

Nothing more I imagine need be faid, to demon-
ftrate the unreafonablenefs and inexpediency of any meafure tending to continue the agency on its prefent footing. But independent of all other objections, I object
to the propofed contract, as to an act exceeding the limits
of our lawful authority.

If it be in the power of a majority of this board, at
the moment of their own diffolution, to bind their fucceffors by engagements for any term they think proper,
and to difable them from correcting any exifting abufe,
it will be in vain for the Company or Parliament to
change the adminiftration of the Company's affairs in the
country, and to veft it in other hands. That queftion
however, if I continue in the government, fhall be tried

F 2

in

in behalf of the Company; and if it be in my power, the exorbitant profits of this agency, in whatever shape it may be continued, shall be reduced. In the mean time, I protest against the proposition, and will not sign the contract.

(Signed) P. FRANCIS.

Mr. Barwell,

I have read with attention, the dissent and protest of Mr. Francis to the measure for continuing the supply of victualling stores with Mr. Belli, the present agent, who furnishes these stores.

The principles on which this dissent is grounded, might require examination, if the warmth with which it is made, and the intimation given in the concluding words of it, would allow any one who reads it, to doubt the influence under which it is written.

That species of disposition, which is established and maintained by the operation of an unremitted dependence on the will of rulers, is, of all others, most pernicious to a community, because every member of a community so circumstanced, must, when it systematically prevails, either preserve his station by servile compliances, or risk it by venturing to act on principles of freedom. In short, unremitted dependence for pecuniary benefits, is a constant bribe given to an individual, by the rules of every state, who annex it as a condition to the benefit they confer. I cannot therefore acquiesce in the reasoning I have heard advanced by the members in opposition, nor subscribe to their opinion, which would make the present agent, who furnishes and keeps up the deposit of provisions for Fort William, hold his office during pleasure.

The objections which are made to the commission of
fifteen

fifteen per cent. for furnishing the stores, and to the
fifteen per cent. allowed to indemnify the agent for re-
placing the decayed and damaged stores, and for renewing the whole deposit every year, are indeed ingeniously
stated, and the inventive powers appear racked to the
utmost to make this commission, and this allowance,
amounting in the whole to thirty per cent. strike the su-
perficial reader as an exorbitant premium; but I will adventure to affirm on my own knowledge, of the perishable
nature of the stores supplied and kept up, that it is not
possible for the agent to derive much or any benefit, if he
does not suffer a loss, which I really think he must from
this part of his engagement. Where is the garrison in
which a deposit of provisions is kept at the public charge,
that does not condemn more than fifteen per cent. of
such stores in the course of one year; over and above the
heavy loss arising to the public, by the yearly renovation
of the deposit? I believe the depot of the garrison of
Gibraltar is not, nor can be maintained by the English
government at so small an expence, while the supplies are
contracted for, and the loss on condemned stores borne
by the nation, as well as of those which, though not
condemned, are sold off at the end of every year as being
of a perishable nature, and though fit for immediate
use, are not in a state of preservation, or capable of it,
for the course of another season. And if this is the case,
and it certainly is the case, fifteen per cent. for the renovation of the deposit of provisions for Fort William, and
the loss arising from condemned stores, is a very moderate premium, much more moderate, I affirm, than the
expence would be to our government, was a contract
entered into for an annual supply, and the old stores in
preservation and those condemned, sold at the end of
every year for Government. Why it should be advanced
as an argument against the mode proposed for keeping
up a deposit in high and perfect preservation, that the
agent possibly may do it without loss to himself, I cannot
comprehend

comprehend, unlefs it means to affirm, by implication, that Government can keep up fuch a depofit with equal facility, and without lofs, or little lofs. If this is the pofition laboured to be eftablifhed, I deny it, and the experience of every man muft contradict it.

. In what office of our Government, or in any Government, are ftores of a perifhable nature kept up without lofs, and a heavy lofs to Government. I am fure in no office that has ever fallen under my obfervation, and I call upon the other members for information if any office has, under theirs.

In all the offices of fupply under our Government, advances are made on the application of our officers, and a commiffion of fifteen per cent. allowed on the rates fixed by Government on the articles to be fupplied. On many articles this commiffion is reduced to nothing; as their real price far exceeds the rates—while on others it is enhanced by being below the rates. I dare affirm the agent for keeping up the depofit of provifion for Fort William, would efteem himfelf very happy to draw his commiffion clear for the fupplies, and difengage himfelf from the further allowance of fifteen per cent. with the condition annexed to it, of renewing and keeping up the depofit. But as I am convinced it is not for the intereft of Government to remit this condition, and contract at fifteen per cent. fimply for an annual fupply, I can never acquiefce to make his office a mere office of fupply, and fubject the Company to the burthenfome lofs of renewing yearly fuch perifhable ftores; the perplexed and intricate manner in which the account annexed to Mr. Francis's minute is drawn, obliges me to oppofe to it a more fimple and comprehenfive one, fhewing the periods; the amount of the fupplies, and the commiffion, to the 1ft of May, 1779, from the 1ft of May, 1777, in which period the firft purchafe of 150,231r. 8a. 3p.

muft

muſt have been renewed twice at the expence of the agent, and the ſubſequent ones to the thirtieth of April once.

I will not propoſe that the commiſſion drawn of fifteen per cent. in the courſe of the ſame period ſhould ſtand oppoſed—I am convinced none of the other offices of ſupply are ſo low, or in which the ſervices of the agents have a meaner reward.

I agree to the propoſition for keeping up a depoſit of proviſions for the garriſon of Fort William, on the terms of the exiſting agency on a contract for five years.

The Governor General deſires the following Minute may be recorded on the proceedings in reply to Mr. Francis's of the 17th of Auguſt:

Mr. Barwell has already ſo fully anſwered every objection urged by Mr. Francis, againſt the propriety of continuing to Mr. Belli, the agency for ſupplying the garriſon of Fort William in proviſions for five years, that any further remarks from me appear to be unneceſſary, but when I conſider Mr. Belli's ſituation in my family, and the acrimony of ſtile diſplayed in Mr. Francis's proteſt, as well as the ſeveral inſinuations contained in it, I cannot help deeming the violent oppoſition he has made to my motion, as perſonal; and viewing it in this light, I ſhall trouble the board with a few remarks upon the ſubject, after having thankfully acknowledged how much I think myſelf obliged to Mr. Barwell (*whatever were his motives*)[1] both for the readineſs and ability with which he has refuted the arguments offered by Mr. Francis againſt this meaſure.

Mr.

. Mr. Francis begins by obferving, that this contract
is in direct oppofition to the Company's orders, and
that the bufinefs has hitherto been performed . by
agency, &c.

To furnifh a depofit of provifions for the garrifon
of Fort William, is not bufinefs for proclamation, nor
to be difpofed of to the loweft bidder, for the reafons
which I before ufed, and which Mr. Francis, I know
not why, has quoted againft it.

An agency with a fixed rate, and a fixed commifion,
is to all intents and purpofes a contract. All that I
have now propofed is, to fix the term, and to bind the
contract by penalties.

I can by no means agree with Mr. Francis, that the
agent victualler enjoys the moft profitable employment
that ever exifted in this government.

*Mr. Livius has an agency with 15 per cent. commiffion
on articles rated by former charges of commiffaries, of
courfe greatly above the real coft. Mr. Livius is profeffedly patronized by Mr. Francis, who paffes his bills.—
Nine or ten lacks thus paid to him, are yet unaccounted
for.*

In an anfwer to Mr. Francis's infinuation, that it
is natural enough for the agent to wifh to fecure himfelf, before the expiration of the prefent government, *I avow the fact as to myfelf, as well as to the
agent.*

When I fee a fyftematic oppofition to every meafure
propofed by me for the fervice of the public, by
which an individual may eventually benefit, I cannot
hefitate a moment to declare it to be my firm belief,
that

that fhould the government of this country be placed
in the hands of the prefent minority, they would feek
the ruin of every man connected with me. *It is
therefore only an act of common juftice in me, to wifh to
fecure them, as far as I legally can, from the apprehenfion
of future oppreffion.*

Mr. Francis has grofsly mif-ftated my minute, when
he fays, I affirm the contractor has fuftained heavy
loffes, by the indefinite term of his agency. I am
forry to add this to the many inftances upon record,
during the courfe of our debates, of the inaccuracy of
Mr. Francis's quotations, and his fubfequent reafonings
in confequence.

I faid he was " *fubjected to many heavy loffes, and
fome he has actually fuftained in the purchafe of articles at*
20 per cent. above the table of rates;" on the capital
article of grain, he has indeed been a gainer, his purchafes having been luckily made at a time of plenty,
and his fales, with the public apprehenfion of a fcarcity.
His fuccefs in this inftance has alarmed him for the
future, and with reafon.

Suppofe the reverfe had happened, with his indefinite agency, which may expire to-morrow, he can
only venture to purchafe what is immediately wanted,
and that he is obliged to provide. He cannot venture
to inveft a large capital in diftant commiffions. Of
courfe his purchafes, by being made at hand, are from
the deareft, as well as the neareft markets. He may
buy his rice at 20 feers for the rupee; he may be under the neceffity of felling it at 40, and this one article
proves his ruin.

With what propriety can the profits of this agency
be ftiled immoderate?

G

The

The rates were fixed by accurate and actual rates of the market, and the agent was allowed the cuftomary commiffion of 15 per cent. on the purchafes, he was obliged to change the ftores, and allowed for damages (which in many would be the lofs of the whole, and in all of fomething) 15 per cent. on the prime coft, fo fold. This Mr. Francis calls 30 per cent. and rates it as a clear profit.—Befides this drawback, the agent, as will appear from an infpection of his books, if called for, has frequently been obliged to purchafe ftores at a price far exceeding the allowances made to him by the Company.

In the purchafe of

Ghee, he loft	20	per cent.
Moong — —	25	ditto
Turmerick — —	17½	ditto
Oil — —	52	ditto
Salt beef — —	33	ditto

He is likewife liable to loffes in the tranfportation of goods to Calcutta, and by an adventure from Purnea laft feafon, fuftained a lofs of 10,000 rupees.

Mr. Francis, ftating the fum of current rupees 2,29,912, as a clear gain to the agent, makes no deduction for the loffes I have fpecified, nor has he confidered the decay, waftage, fervants wages, cooley hire, and other unavoidable expences, attending the agency for near three years; but in order to fwell this fum as much as poffible, he has included in it, about 70,000 rupees, as received by the agent, though the rifk for which it was paid to him will not expire 'till May, 1780.

Mr. Francis once thought differently of my plan:
the

the words of his minute delivered on the 4th November, 1776, when it was firſt read at the Board, were, " *If the ſervice be neceſſary in any degree, it is a ſervice of the firſt neceſſity, and ſhould not be ſtinted for the ſake of any inconſiderable ſaving, which in the event perhaps might only be apparent.*"

I am firmly of opinion, and am happy to be confirmed in it by the ſentiments of the commander in chief, that the ſervice muſt continue of the firſt neceſſity, while we continue in poſſeſſion of Fort William.

I alſo moſt heartily concur with the commander in chief in opinion, that the Board could not confer a contraĉt of this importance on a gentleman of more honor and integrity than Mr. Belli, or who could more conſcientiouſly diſcharge the duties of it.

In reply to Mr. Francis's obſervation, *that Mr. Belli enjoys the favor and protećtion of government*, I do moſt ſolemnly declare that he has never applied to me for the moſt trifling interference or ſupport in his agency.

I have one remark to make on the ſubjeĉt of this agency ſince Mr. Francis has thought proper to make ſo pointed an attack upon it. He muſt remember how ſtrenuoſly it was oppoſed by the late General Clavering in its ſeveral ſtages. His proteſts and remarks were tranſmitted to the Court of Directors, and were received at a time when our proceedings were rigidly ſcrutinized, and when every meaſure propoſed by me which could be deemed in the ſmalleſt degree objećtionable, underwent the ſevereſt comment.

My plan for ſupplying Fort William with proviſions, paſſed without a remark; and this is to me a

G 2 convincing

convincing proof that the Directors esteemed it to be highly beneficial to the company*.

(Signed) WARREN HASTINGS.

Houghly, 2d October, 1779.

Mr. Francis,

I HAVE not seen Mr. Barwell's minute in which the Governor General affirms, that *every objection* urged by me against the contract proposed to be given to Mr. Belli for five years, is fully answered. I did not know that such a minute existed; and unless facts can be altered, I cannot for my own part conceive it possible, that mine can be refuted. The Governor General's minute was transmitted to me this morning.

If recrimination does not imply an admission of the charge, it certainly is no defence against it; I cannot allow that one abuse is justified by another; nor am I bound to answer any objections, whether valid or not, to the agency for stores held by Mr. Livius.—The Governor General and Mr. Barwell had just as much concern in giving it to him as I had.—*If it be liable to abuse, why is it not corrected? if his profits are too great, why have they not been reduced? Mr. Hastings and Mr. Barwell have had absolute power in their hands for above three years.*

It is said " *that Mr. Livius has an agency with fifteen per cent. commission on articles rated by former charges of commissaries; of course greatly above the real cost.*" If the

_____

* Yet the Directors have severely censured it, in their letter by the General Barker; but being slow in their proceedings, it encouraged Mr. Hastings to infer in his own favour, that they had approved it.

the affertion were true in terms, it remains to be explained, even on the principle of precedents, *how the giving fifteen per cent. to one agent, juftifies giving thirty per cent. to another.*—Meff. Robinfon, Killican, and Croftes reported that 20 per cent. per ann. would be a reafonable commiffion to Mr. Belli. *Mr. Haftings and Mr. Barwell, neverthelefs gave him thirty.*—With refpeƈt to the military ftorekeeper's book of rates, the faƈt is, *that it was formed by the late Colouel Dow, with the approbation of the Board of Ordnance, not by the former charge of the commiffaries, but by an enquiry into the aƈtual Bazar prices of that period;* whether Mr. Livius gains or lofes by thofe rates, is unknown to me. I believe that occafionally he may do both.—I have no right to examine his mercantile books, nor does it concern the fervice in queftion.

It is faid that " *Mr. Livius is profeffedly patronized by me,*" I recommended him to the office of military ftorefteeper, and I would maintain him in the juft rights belonging to it, on the fame principle, on which I would infift on his performing the duties of it; thus far my patronage of Mr. Livius has extended.

But it is faid, " *that I pafs his bills* ;" the affertion, as it ftands expreffed, may be fuppofed to be a miftake.—The Governor well knows, that I refigned the employment of comptroller of the offices from the end of December, 1778; and that I have repeatedly urged to him the neceffity of requefting fome other member of the board to undertake it from that period. Places of influence and profit, are not feen fo eafily relinquifhed. If the accounts of the public offices have not fince been examined, the Governor General, I prefume, will affign his reafons for it to the company; neither is it true, that I ever paffed Mr. Livius's bill in the fenfe plainly implied by the Governor:

they

they were conftantly examined by Mr. Baugh and his
affiftant, with the utmoft ftrictnefs, before they came
to me for their final confirmation.   My diary is before
the Court of Directors, it was not poffible therefore,
that I could favour Mr. Livius, or any body elfe,
unlefs Mr. Baugh and I acted in collufion,   I defire
that he may be examined at the board upon his oath,
and in my abfence, concerning the manner in which I
executed my part of the examination ; and I moft ear-
neftly requeft of Mr. Wheler, to make a motion in my
behalf to this effect, at the next Board of Infpection:
I leave it to the Governor General and Mr. Barwell to
put fuch queftions to him as they think fit.   It would
be much beneath me to make any other reply to the
conclufion evidently meant to be drawn from the fuppofed fact " *of my paffing Mr. Livius's bills,*" but that
I receive it as it deferves.

Again it is afferted, " *that nine or ten lacks thus paid
to Mr. Livius, are yet unaccounted for.*"   I do not
know what the amount of the military ftore-keeper's
difburfements may be fince December laft, having no
concern in the examination of his accounts. - The
fecretary has the monthly accounts before him, and I
defire he will ftate the amount in this place, (current
R's.   A.   P.
rupees 4,18,965 : 13 : 6) the military ftore-keeper's
accounts of his difburfements being given unto him
every month, and a balance ftruck before he receives a
farther advance for the enfuing month, it cannot truly
be faid, that the fums he has received fince December
laft, are unaccounted for.   If his accounts are not examined, it is not his fault.

Any perfon unacquainted with the tranfaction of
bufinefs in the military ftore-keeper's office, and who
faw only in what circumftances, and with what apparent

parent view it is afferted, " *that nine or ten lacks thus paid to Mr. Livius, fince December laft, are yet unaccounted for,*" would naturally conclude that this money was all on account of his agency for the provifion of military ftores. For if it were not fo, the comparifon between his fuppofed profits, and thofe of Mr. Belli (to fhelter which, Mr. Livius's name and office are manifeftly introduced) proves nothing, and falls to the ground. Now the faft is, that the greateft part of the monthly fums iffued to Mr. Livius, are advanced to him as military ftore-keeper, not as agent. Out of thefe he pays his own office charges by a fixed eftablifh-ment; the eftablifhment of the commiffary general's office, with the price of all the articles furnifhed by Lieutenant Colonel Green by contract; the price of all the powder furnifhed monthly by the powder con-tractor; and many other contingencies. In the ma-nagement of all thefe difburfements, the military ftore-keeper pays as faft as he receives, and has no profit whatfoever, not even that of having a fum of public money for a fhort time in his hands. It is a faft, not unworthy of notice in this place, that all the other heads of officers, receive their monthly advances twenty days before he does, owing to fome difficulty of adjuftment between him and the Commiffary; by which in this refpect they both fuffer.

The following ftatement which I have defired the fecretary to fill up, will fhew what proportion the fore-going difburfements, bear to the total amount of the military ftore-keeper's advances, fince December laft.

Firft, Total amount of advances, from January, 1779, inclufive   *Current Rupees.* 442105 : 7 : 6

Second

Second, Amount of office charges,
- as per establishment for ditto — 6899 : 8 : o

Third, Amount paid to Lieutenant
Colonel Green, for ditto — 163213:7 : 8

Fourth, Ditto to the powder contractor — — — — 124605 14 : 9

Five, Ditto of all other contingent
expences — — — — 122116 : 2 : 10

Total Current Rupees 2,69,943 : 1 : 3

Difference 1,72,162 : 6 : 3

To that part of the Governor General's minute
which immediately follows, I shall make no answer.
He supposes his facts, and draws his conclusion from
them. Perhaps we ought to deem it a proof of his
moderation, that he has not endeavoured to secure his
friends in the possession of all the lucrative contracts,
as well as employments, for the next twenty years; and
that he has confined the intended operation of his influence to so short a period as five years, after the expiration of his administration. He had full as good a
right to do one as the other.

I have quoted the Governor General's own words at
length; yet he says, " *that I have grossly mis-stated his minute.*" At the worst, I could only have been guilty of
a misconstruction, of which every man, who reads my
minute, would be able to judge, having the Governor's
words literally quoted before him; I did really conceive
that it was meant to be asserted, or understood at least,
that Mr. Belli had suffered heavy losses and inconveniencies,

niencies. It did not occur to me, that he could have made *" frequent remonstrances concerning the heavy losses and inconveniencies to which he was subjected by the present indefinite term of his agency."* If, in fact, and after an experience of near two years, he had suffered no such losses and inconveniences, we are therefore to attribute these frequent remonstrances of the agent, not to any losses and inconveniences he has actually sustained, but merely to the quickness of his apprehension. He finds himself subjected to losses, of which hitherto he had no experience, and nothing less than a contract for five years can secure him against them.

Here one would think we might be sure of our facts, and that the argument might be concluded. The Governor General, however, is pleased to take new ground; after charging me with having *" grossly misstated his minute,"* in the construction I gave to the words, *" subjected to many heavy losses,"* he himself now asserts, that *" some he has actually sustained."* The word *" some,"* I presume, must refer to *heavy losses*; and, if that be true, my construction of his original words is no other than what he himself now gives them, and confirms; if not, he must be understood to have intended to weaken his own argument, by saying, that the agent was only liable to heavy losses, when he might have said, as he does now, that he had actually suffered them.

I have stated the whole commission as a clear gain to the agent, from a conviction, that it was, or might have been so, or within a mere trifle of it. In the supply of articles of provision, the bazar market retail rates of Calcutta are the highest that could be taken. A contractor, who purchases in gross quantities in the different parts of the country in which the articles are produced, ought to gain at least enough between the purchase and the Company's price, to defray all charges of merchandize

H and

and other expences whatfoever, confidering always that he trades with the public money, and not with his own.

The plan to which I originally gave my affent, was propofed at a time when I thought that an invafion of thefe provinces was a probable event. That apprehenfion, whether well or ill-founded, was the ground of this and feveral other opinions delivered by me, tending to prove the expediency, if not neceffity, of putting thefe provinces in a pofture of defence. The Governor General conftantly treated the idea of an invafion as chimerical; yet, in this inftance, as well as in many others, in which our military and naval eftablifhments have been, on his principles, very unneceffarily augmented, he acted as if he thought the apprehenfion of an invafion was not ill-founded; his opinion has been juftified by the event, but they both condemn his conduct.

I never would ftint a neceffary fervice for the fake of any inconfiderable faving. I thought this a neceffary fervice at the time when it was propofed, and I would not have ftinted it; not that I difregard little favings, but becaufe I know, by experience, that while they are attended to, the great ones are neglected. But admitting that the circumftances of public affairs were not changed, as I affirm they are, is this really the fame plan to which I originally gave my confent? Did I ever confent to allow the agent a commiffion of thirty per cent. per annum againft the opinion of the merchants to whom the reference was made, and whofe opinion was to have decided the queftion? On the contrary, did I not remonftrate againft it? Was the binding the India Company by contract to maintain a fpecific garrifon in Fort William, and in one particular mode, and whether they approved of it or not, and under every poffible change of the circumftances of the government, ever fuggefted to me at the time the agency was propofed? If thefe queftions cannot

not be anfwered in the affirmative, it follows, that it is not I who think differently of the plan, but the Governor General, who has changed his plan for a purpofe in which the public fervice has no concern.

On the remainder of the Governor's minute I fhall make no remarks, though not for want of materials; I content myfelf with doing my own duty, and leave it to others to anfwer for themfelves.

(Signed)   P. FRANCIS.

On the 6th of October, 1779.

SIR,

I defire you will fend the inclofed minute in circulation. I remain, Sir, your's,

E. WHELER.

In confequence of the moft earneft requeft of Mr. Francis, I move, that Mr. Baugh may be examined at the board upon oath, concerning the manner in which Mr. Francis hath examined and paffed the accounts of Mr. George Livius. And I muft further defire, that his (Mr. Baugh's) examination may be taken in Mr. Francis's abfence.

E. W.

Extract Confultation the 1ft of November, 1779.

Mr. Baugh attending the board in confequence of the motion made by Mr. Wheeler, and entered in the laft confultation, is admitted.

H 2   Read

Read – The motion of Mr. Wheeler.

Mr. Francis.—My intention was, to give the Governor General an opportunity of satisfying himself, and doing me justice, upon the points alluded to in the motion. I do not infist upon his oath, becaufe I am perfectly fatisfied that his teftimony will be equally valid without it. As I was fick at Houghly at the time the motion was made, I did imagine it would be refolved upon in my abfence, but I have no difficulty about its being determined now.

Governor General.—I fhall put no queftions to Mr. Baugh in the mode prefcribed; I think it very irregular. I have not even given Mr. Francis's minute an intire perufal, although I have kept it by me for fome time with the intention of examining it, and of replying to it, if I had found it neceffary. Other bufinefs of more importance, a ftrong averfion to perfonal debate, and a conviction of its inutility for any purpofe, either of decifion here, or of reference at home, have hitherto concurred to make me poftpone it. Mr. Baugh is now before the board at the requifition of Mr. Francis. I fhall leave it to Mr. Francis to put what queftions he may think proper to him, either upon oath, or otherwife.

Mr. Wheeler.—I am called upon by Mr. Francis to take a part in this difagreeable bufinefs, which is exceedingly irkfome to myfelf, and becomes ftill more fo by the Governor General's declining to put any queftions to Mr. Baugh. If time had permitted a fhort anfwer to Mr. Francis's laft minute, it might have anfwered the fame purpofe as the queftions which I muft now addrefs to Mr. Baugh, and I doubt not but the anfwers will give the board every fatisfaction they can require.

Mr.

Mr. *Wheeler* delivers the following queſtions to be put to Mr. Baugh.

1ſt. Whether it is not your duty, as aſſiſtant to the comptroller of the offices, to examine the monthly accounts of each office before they are ſeen by the comptroller, and to furniſh him with whatever remarks may have occurred to you thereon ?

Anſwer. Preparatory to the comptroller's examining the accounts of the offices, they have always been examined by my aſſiſtant, ſo far as reſpected their calculations and additions, after which they have been compared by me, with the vouchers delivered with them. I have then compared ſuch charges as were eſtabliſhed, with the fixed eſtabliſhments ; alſo ſuch charges for ſtores provided by contract, or by agency, with the terms of the different engagements for thoſe ſupplies. And if upon this examination I have diſcovered any deviation from either, I have pointed them out to the Comptroller, who has either immediately deducted the difference, or applied to the head of that department, whoſe accounts were under examination, for an explanation.

2nd. Whether you have not conſtantly done ſo ?

Anſwer. Yes, I have.

3d. Whether you have ever obſerved, that Mr. Francis, in examining the accounts of the military ſtore keeper, or of any other of the public offices, or in paſſing their bills, or in any other inſtance whatſoever, has favoured the military ſtore keeper, or any other perſon, or has ever ſuffered an error or overcharge in his or their accounts, to paſs without correction and cenſure ?

Governor

Governor General.—I beg that Mr. Baugh may be difpenfed from anfwering the third queftion, if there is a neceffity for it; it is highly improper on many accounts, confidering the wide diftance between Mr. Baugh and Mr. Francis, that he fhould be obliged to anfwer to fuch a queftion. *I do not recollect what words of mine have given occafion for it; but if I have made ufe of any, which either directly lay fuch a charge to Mr. Francis's account, or imply it, I retract them, without accounting at this time for the manner in which any fuch expreffions may have efcaped me, as they are now entirely out of my memory. The object of the queftion therefore is removed.*

Mr. Francis.—I am fatisfied, and defire the queftion may be waved.

4th. To what point of time have the military ftore keeper's accounts been examined and paffed by the Comptroller?

Anfw. To the end of December, 1778.

5th. What is the amount of the monthly fums iffued to and from the treafury for the monthly difburfements of his office, including his agency fince December 1778, to the end of September laft?

Anfw. The advances made to the military ftore keeper from the treafury, between the 1ft of January and 30th of September, 1779, amount to current rupees 4,24,000; but in this fum is not included his advance on account of September, being 42,000 rupees, becaufe it did not pafs the board in time to be iffued during that month. The order of the treafury was not figned till t   h of September; and I obferve, by the eftimate c   's difburfements for October, that the
    cived till the 6th of the laft-mentioned month.

month. In Mr. Francis's minute of the 2nd of October, the amount of the advances issued to the military store keeper to the end of August, is stated by me at current rupees 4,42,105 : 7 : 6 ; but it is proper to remark, that in this sum is included the monthly payments made to him by Mr. Robert Stewart, on account of the new powder works, and his receipts for ready money sales.

6th. Has the military store keeper delivered in his monthly accounts regularly to the Comptroller's office since December last ?

Answ. Yes, to the end of September.

Governor General.—I desire to put the two following questions to Mr. Baugh.

1st. Have Mr. Livius's accounts ever appeared before the board ?

2d. What is the amount of Mr. Livius's receipts and disbursements, from the time he first had charge of his present office, to the date of my minute in September ? If Mr. Baugh cannot answer the last of these questions from his own official knowledge, I desire him to obtain proper official information to compleat his answer ?

1st *Answ.* They never have appeared before the board. It was not the intent of the regulations constituting the Comptroller's office, that they should be laid before the board.

2d *Answ.* Not having the necessary materials in my possession for furnishing the accounts required by the Governor General, I applied for it to the military store keeper, and beg leave to lay before the board the fol-

lowing

lowing abſtracts, which I have in conſequence received
from him, of his recepts and diſburſements from April
1775 to September, 1779, incluſive, the former amounting to current rupees 23,16,074 : 13 : 3 ; the latter
to 23,1678 : 1 : 3, which conſtituted a balance in favour of Mr. Livius, which he had actually advanced for
the Company, inſtead of being nine or ten lacks in ar-
rear.. Mr. Livius was appointed to the office of military
ſtore keeper on the 20th of March, 1775, and the Governor's minute is dated in September, 1779.

I think it proper to acquaint the board, that my application for this account would have been made to the
Accomptant General, and not to the military ſtore
keeper, could the former have furniſhed it complete.
But the general books being balanced only to the 30th
of April, 1778, it could not have been prepared from
them to a period ſubſequent to that time. I believe
alſo, that the entries in the general books are adjuſted
from the abſtracts of the receipts and diſburſements ſup-
plied to the Accomptant General by the heads of the
different offices.

Minutes

Minutes on the Advance Salary and Appointment to Sir Eyre Coote. Extract Board of Inspection the 12th of April, 1779.

Read the following propositions of Lieutenant General Sir Eyre Coote.

That the five half shares of the revenue do devolve upon Sir Eyre Coote, as Commander in Chief, from his arrival in Fort William on the 23d of March, and that General Stibbert do only share as oldest Colonel from that time.

That the 3000 rupees per month, lately granted to General Stibbert for contingent expences in the field, do devolve on General Coote, from the 31st of March, as Commander in Chief.

That the 16,000 rupees per annum, for secret intelligence, do devolve to General Sir Eyre Coote from the 31st of March.

Sir Eyre Coote delivers in the following minute.

The reference I made to the board on the subject of General Stibbert's allowances, which exceed mine by 82,750 rupees per annum, proceeded from an idea, that they were granted to him as Commander in Chief, under the presidency; and as, on my arrival at Fort William, he could be no longer considered in that capacity, whatever he drew under such a denomination must necessarily be discontinued to him.

An examination of the minutes of Council has rendered me master of the several reasons assigned for granting him those allowances; and my researches on

I

this

this occasion have led me also to a knowledge of the sentiments which have been expressed by the members of the board in general, respecting the insufficiency of the salary allowed by the Court of Directors to their Commander in Chief in India.

From a long experience of the service, I am thoroughly convinced of the justice of this opinion, and I am equally certain, that the Court of Directors never meant I should suffer in my private fortune by carrying on the public service.

You will please therefore, Gentlemen, to adopt such measures as may prevent any unnecessary expence from falling on the Company, and which will at the same time enable me to execute the duties incumbent upon me, as their Commander in Chief, to visit the several stations of the troops, or to take the field, if necessary, without involving myself in expences, which I should be unable to support.

(Signed)   E. COOTE.

Mr. Francis,

I have prepared my opinion on the Commander in Chief's propositions, and beg leave to lay it before the board.

My opinion on the account of General Stibbert's allowances is very fully stated in the consultation of the 14th of May, 1778, and I adhere to it in every particular. I think they should now be reduced to the establishment at which they stood during General Clavering's command. This establishment was formerly referred to the Company, and confirmed by them in their letter of the 24th of December, 1776, paragraph 49.—I

cannot

cannot confent to any variation from the allowances,
fixed by, and enjoyed by General Clavering, without
the Company's orders.—The very laſt which they have
given, and which Sir Eyre Coote brought out with
him, direct, that Lieutenant General Sir Eyre Coote
do receive the ſame pay as Commander in Chief of their
forces in India as was received by Lieutenant General
Sir John Clavering. If all the allowances ſtated in the
propoſitions are agreed to, the preſent Commander in
Chief will receive eighty-two thouſand two hundred
current rupees per annum more than was received by
his predeceſſor.

(Signed)   P. FRANCIS.

Mr. Barwell,

AS I expect in a ſhort time the orders of the Company on the additional allowances drawn by Brigadier
General Stibbert, there does not appear any urgent neceſſity to proceed on the regulation of ſuch allowances
until the arrival of the Company's inſtructions. The
Court of Directors, in fixing the eſtabliſhed ſalary for a
commander of all their forces in India, have expreſſed
it as a ſalary. They therefore certainly intend it to be
drawn free, and diſburthened from all diſburſements to
be incurred in the immediate execution of their military
ſervice; they certainly did not intend to put the Commander in Chief of all their military forces upon a
meaner eſtabliſhment than the provincial Commander
in Chief at the other preſidencies, or General Stibbert,
whoſe allowance by the 49th paragraph of their letter of
the 24th of December, 1776, is reckoned at 82,000
rupees. Theſe facts are ſo very ſtriking, that I cannot
doubt of our having full authority to regulate an eſtabliſhment for Sir Eyre Coote, while in the field, as may
be ſuitable to his high rank, and bear ſome proportion

I 2   to

to the allowances made to the fubordinate field officers
of this government: I am for the queftion, that a field
eftablifhment be formed for Lieutenant General Coote,
Commander in Chief of all the Company's forces while
in the field.

Governor General,

THE allowance of five half fhares of the commiffion
on, the revenues was not an eftablifhment annexed to
his ftation, but a bounty fpecially and perfonally
granted to General Stibbert, by the order of the Court
of Directors in the 31ft paragraph of their general
letter of the 16th of April, 1777. It cannot, therefore, be taken from him, but by the fame authority.

The allowance of 3000 rupees per month for contingent expences in the field was granted to General
Stibbert by a feparate act of this board, though their
refolutions upon this fubject have been various, yet the
opinions of the different members, refpecting the neceffity of fuch an allowance, have been generally the
fame, as may be feen by the proceedings of the board
of the 29th of February, 1776, when this fubject was
firft brought under the confideration of the board, and
for other reafons rejected. For the truth of this, I ap-
peal particularly to the opinions of General Clavering
and Colonel Monfon.

This was never meant as an allowance annexed to
the ftation of Commander in Chief, for when it was
firft propofed, General Stibbert was not confidered as
invefted with that character, but to defray the unavoidable expence attendant on the command in the field.

As the refolution of the board upon this fubject has
been long fince referred to the Court of Directors, with
another

another relative circumstance, which must force their attention to it, and draw from them a clear decision upon it; and as that decision may be expected with the first difpatches of the feafon, I think it would be improper and irregular to make any alteration in it at this time.

I do not recollect any orders which authorifes General Stibbert to draw a fixed fum for fecret fervice. This is an expence in its nature variable, and the Court of Directors, in their letter of the 24th of December, 1776, have exprefsly directed that it shall not be fixed, but that Colonel Stibbert, (that is commander in the field) shall be paid fuch expences as shall appear to us to have been necefsarily incurred by him, from time to time, on that account.

I apprehend, that this is a fervice which will properly and exclufively belong to the Commander in Chief, whenever his fituation will enable him to affume the charge of it, and that General Stibbert should be accordingly directed to conform to his orders refpecting it.

Refpecting the incidental charges of the Commander in Chief, when he is in the field, or which in this point will be equivalent, when he is abfent from the prefidency, I shall premife the following obfervations:

1ft, The prefent allowances drawn by General Stibbert is as follows:

Pays Brigadier General, 750l. per ann.   7,500
Table expences in the field ———   60,000
Contingent expences in the field   —   36,000
Commission in the revenue, current ru-
    pees, 121,368, or   —   —   19,250
                           Sonat Rupees 1,22,750

I do not reckon the allowance for secret service, because I regard it as a public charge, in which he has
no interest, or other concern, than faithfully to disburse
what he draws.

Of the above establishment the following sums have
been allotted to General Stibbert, by the express appointment of the Court of Directors:

Pay as Brigadier General   —   —   7,500
Table charges in the field   —   60,000
Commission on the revenue at that time,
    as I find it computed in Mr. Francis's
    minute of the 14th of May, 1778, cur-
    rent rupees 24,486, or   —   22,059
                          Sonat Rupees 89,559

The salary allowed to the Commander in Chief, by
the fundamental regulations of this government, is
6000l. per annum, or rupees 60,000.

The sum is expressed to be in lieu of all charges and
contingencies in the field ; but the Court of Directors
have since granted to their first Colonel on this establishment, as I have remarked above, an annual stipend
of 80,559 rupees, a sum exceeding that of a Commander in Chief by nearly 50 per cent.

                                              But

But it cannot be fuppofed, that the Court of Directors ever meant to invert the order of the fervice, and that in fo great a degree, as to make a partial and unjuft diftinction between an officer placed, not by felection, but by cafual fucceffion, at the head of a fingle eftablifhment, and the Commander in Chief of all the Britifh forces in India; therefore, when they paffed thefe grants to Colonel, now General, Stibbert, they *virtually* eftablifhed a precedent for a proportionate augmentation of the allowances of the Commander in Chief of all the Britifh forces in India; for it cannot be difputed, that his unavoidable expences in the difcharge of all the various duties annexed to his ftation muft greatly exceed thofe of General Stibbert in a limitted command; and I will prefume, that had it been at the fame time propofed to afcertain the allowances of the Commander in Chief, they would have augmented them proportionably.

On the premifed grounds, I move,

1ft. That the Commander in Chief be allowed to draw for the expences of his table, when he is in the field, 90,000 rupees per annum.

2. That the Commander in Chief be authorized to draw for the following eftablifhment for himfelf and his ftaff, when he is in the field, in lieu of travelling, and all incidental charges whatever.

12 Budge-

12 Budgerows	—	150	—	1800
30 Boats	—	40	—	1200
10 Elephants	—	75	—	750
200 Coolies	—	5	—	1000
28 Hircarahs	—	7	—	196
1 Head ditto	—	30	—	30
1 Naib	—	15	—	15
				4991
50 Lascars	—	8	—	400
1 Serang	—	20	—	20
2 Tindals	—	15	—	30
4 Hackeries	—	30	—	120
2 Gurry Men	—	7	—	15
2 Writers	—		—	150
Stationary	—		—	200
12 Horses	—		—	360

S. Rs. 6286

The sums which I have annexed to the establishment are added merely to shew the computed amount of it, but are not taken from any correct authority, nor meant to be a part of the proposition. If this motion shall be agreed to, it will be the province of the Commissary General to affix the rates of expence to each article, and I shall propose that they be referred to him for that purpose.

Mr. Francis,

On the principles on which the opinion I have already given was founded, I have much more reason to object to the establishment now proposed, than to the Commander in Chief's first propositions. All the allowances granted to General Stibbert, as Commander in in Chief, or otherwife, and which I have conftantly objected to as exceffive, are to be continued to him; and, at the fame time, a total new eftablifhment created, amounting to the monthly charge of current

R. A. P.   R. A.

rupees, 15,302 : 7 : 5. or 1,83,629 : 8 per annum. I am againft the motion *.

Mr. Barwell,

I cannot concur in opinion with Mr. Francis, that the propofed eftablifhment is a double one. I do not underftand thefe allowances are to be drawn upon any other occafion, than that for which it was expreffed, for the General's expences in the field. There is no immediate call, that I know of, upon the Commander in Chief to leave the prefidency†; and, before a month is paff'd, we fhall, in all probability, receive the orders of the Court of Directors, whether Brigadier General Stibbert is to draw the allowances which he is intitled to receive, or whether they are to ceafe.—In either cafe, the neceffity of the eftablifhment now propofed for the Commander in Chief of all the Company's forces is but a fingle eftablifhment, nor is this a monthly eftablifhment, or if it was, is it of the extent ftated? It is an eftablifhment only to be drawn when the public fervice calls the Commander in Chief from the prefidency. That it will be drawn, I admit; but it is not probable it will be drawn through the whole year; befides, it is a charge limited to a fpecific fum, but does not neceffarily include the expenditure of the whole amount.—I agree to the propofition.

Governor General.—I agree to the propofition.

---

* He left it, however, in a fhort time thereafter, and has taken care not to return in a hurry; it was originally underftood to be fo.

† He was afterwards allowed 1200 rupees per month in addition to the above allowance.

Refolved,

Refolved, that the Commander in Chief of the Company's forces in India, be allowed to draw for the expences of his table, when he is in the field, the monthly fum of feven thoufand five hundred Sonat rupees, or ninety thoufand current rupees per annum.

Refolved, That the Commander in Chief of the Company's forces in India, be allowed to draw for the following monthly eftablifhment for himfelf and his ftaff when he is in the field, in lieu of travelling and all incidental charges whatever, when in the field.

12 Budgerows
30 Boats
10 Elephants
200 Coolies
28 Hircarahs
1 Head ditto
1 Naib
50 Lafcars
1 Serang
2 Tindals
4 Hackeries
2 Gurrymen
Stationary
12 Horfes.

Ordered, That this eftablifhment be referred to the Commiffary-General, with directions to affix the rates of expence to each article, fpecified therein.

Mr. Wheeler having delivered the following minute, on the foregoing proceedings being fhewn him by the fecretary, it is entered in this place for the fake of connection.

Mr. *Wheeler* —The argument made ufe of by the Governor-General, to evince the neceffity of an augmentation of allowances to the Commander in Chief

when

when in the field, are by no means sufficient to ob-
obviate those objections, which from a perfect knowledge of the regulations alluded to, suggest themselves to
my mind.

In the first place, the allowances to the commander in
chief by the fundamental regulations of this government,
was not an act of the court of directors, but of the pro-
prietary at large, convened together for that purpose;
and by their orders, communicated to their servants in
Bengal, by the executive part of their constitution, the
court of directors. Thence it appears to me, neither
optional in the court of directors, to encrease or dimi-
nish an allowance voted to their commander in chief by
a general court of proprietors; for if it was, with the
same degree of propriety that the court of directors
could revoke the orders of their constituents by augment-
ing an allowance fixed as above to their commander in
chief, they might revoke any and every act of the proprietors at large.

It naturally follows, that the court of directors do not
in themselves possess the power of altering the allowance
fixed to the office of commander in chief; and it is
equally conclusive with me, that no such power can possibly be vested in our board.

But even admitting their power; it is plain from
the 5th paragraph of their general letter, dated the 7th
of May 1778, by the Stafford, that it was not their intention to deviate from the established allowance, granted
to their late commander.

Without entering therefore into the detail of this
business, or expressing my disapprobation of the enor-
mity of each particular article of increase, I shall content
myself with objecting to any further allowances being
made to Lieutenant General Sir Eyre Coote, that the

court

Court of Directors have in the 60th paragraph of their
letter, dated the 29th of March, 1774, directed to be
paid to Lieutenant-General Sir John Clavering; an
extract of which I shall here subjoin,

" *And that there be paid to him the sum of six thousand*
pounds sterling per annum, in full for his services as com-
mander in chief, and in lieu of travelling charges, and of all
other advantages and emoluments whatever, except his salary
of ten thousand pounds per annum, established by law, and
ordered to be paid him as one of the council at Fort William
in Bengal."

E. WHELER.

Minutes in council, on the treaty with the Rana of
Gohud.

Extract Secret Department Consultation.

November 12th, 1779.

The Governor General informs the board, that
during their late recess, he has had several conferences
with the Minister deputed by the Rana of Gohud;
and invested with full powers on the subject of a treaty
of alliance offensive and defensive, proposed by the
Rana, to be concluded between him and the Company.
The Governor-General lays before the board a draft of
conditions which he has formed on the basis of the
Rana's propositions for such a treaty; and which, with
the Rana's letters and propositions, he desires may be
entered in this place, for the informations and opinions
of the board.

(Signed)   WARREN HASTINGS.

Draft of Treaty.

Article 1st. A treaty of alliance, offensive and defensive

fenfive, fhall be eftablifhed between the Englifh Company and Maha Raja Ranna Lohinder Bahadre.

2d. Whenever a war fhall actually take place between the contracting parties and the Marattas *, if the Rana fhall require the affiftance of an Englifh force for the purpofes hereinafter defcribed, *fuch a force, proportioned to the exigency of the fervice fhall be immediately fent, on his requifition made in writing to the commanding officer at the nearest ftation of the Company's troops; fhall remain with him as long as he fhall require it, and return when he fhall difmifs it* †, the expence thereof fhall be defrayed by the Rana at the fixed rate of twenty thoufand Muchle dar rupees of the currency of Banares, or any other fpecies of rupees of fame intrinfic amount, for each battalion of the Seapoys, on their prefent eftablifhment, with their proportion of artillery §.— The payment to commence on the day when the faid force fhall pafs the borders of the Company's dominions, or the dominions of the Nabob of Oude: and ceafe on the period ftipulated for its return to either; four cofs being allowed for each day's march.

3d. The force fhall be employed for the defence of the Rana's dominions againft all foreign or domeftic enemies, and for the enlargement of his dominions by conqueft on the Marattas.

4th. Whatever acquifition in purfuance of this treaty fhall be made of countries being contiguous to the

---

* The Marattas were then at war with the Rana of Gohud, and his forts attacked.

† Thefe were the ftrange powers to Sujah Dowla, to exterminate the Rohillas.

§ The Rana had not wherewith to pay his own troops.

the Rana's dominions, or formerly appertaining to
them, whether effected by his or the English troops,
separately or in conjunction, or obtained by treaty,
shall be shared in the following proportions, viz. nine
anas to the Company, and seven anas to the Rana:
the mean amount of the gross revenue of the Company's share collected in time of peace in the ten years
preceding, after deducting the charges of collection,
which shall be ascertained by Aumeens chosen by each
party, shall be fixed and paid by the Rana as a perpetual tribute to the Company, and the lands and forts
shall be ceded to the Rana.

5th. In case it shall be judged adviseable to employ the combined forces of the Company and the
Rana in any distant operations against the common
enemy beyond the borders and neighbourhood of the
Rana's dominions, on requisition made in writing from
this government, he shall furnish ten thousand horse
for such service; and each party shall bear his own
separate expence, which shall continue separate until
the return of the combined army to the borders of the
Rana's country, or until it shall be employed in the
services mentioned in the third article of this treaty.

6th. Whenever the English forces are employed
for the defence of the Rana's country, or for the ac-
quisition of territory, the service to be performed shall
be prescribed by himself; but the mode of executing it
shall be left to the direction of the officer commanding
the English troops.

7th. Whenever the combined troops of the Company and the Rana shall be employed in any remote operations, such as are described in the 5th
article, the commanding officers of the English forces
shall consult the Rana on the choice of the service
to

to be performed, but the ultimate decifion, in cafe of a difference of opinion, and the mode of conducting fuch fervice, fhall be left entirely to the commanding officer of the Englifh troops, with a refervation of the Rana's complete authority over his own troops.

8th. Whenever peace fhall be concluded between the Englifh Company and the Maratta ftate, *the Rana fhall be included as a party in the treaty which fhall be made for that purpofe ; and his prefent poffeffions, together with fuch countries as, he fhall have acquired during the courfe of the war, and which it fhall be then ftipulated to leave in his poffeffion, fhall be guarantied to him by fuch treaty**.

9th. No Englifh factory fhall be eftablifhed in the dominions of the Rana. No perfons of any denomination fhall be fent into his dominions, on the part of the Englifh Company, or with the licence of the Governor-General and Council, without his previous confent, nor any authority exercifed over them but his own †.

Ordered, That thefe papers lie for confideration.

Extract Secret Confultation.

2d December, 1779.

Confidered the Governor-General's minute, entered in confultation the 12th of November, with heads

propofed

---

* The Rana is a natural enemy, the Company but an occafional one : yet this treaty of alliance, modeftly engages the Company to compel the ableft power in India, as the only condition of a peace with them, to be reconciled to an irreconcileable enemy. And that that enemy's poffeffions, though incapable of preferving them, fhall be warranted by the Company, at all events.

† Of what benefit will the treaty be to a commercial Company on thefe conditions ?

propofed for a treaty to be concluded with the Rana of Gohud.

Read the letter from the Rana, recorded in the books of the Perfian correfpondence, received the 7th of June laft; alfo another letter dated the 5th of Shaubaun, and received the 3d of September.

Read the propofed heads for a treaty with the Rana of Gohud, entered in confultation the 12th of November.

The Governor-General lays before the board the following amended draft of a treaty propofed to be executed with the Rana of Gohud, and defires that it may be fubftituted for the former, and entered in confultation the 12th ult. As it contains fuch alterations *propofed by the Minifter of the Rana, as the Governor-General deems reafonable.* And to the treaty in this form, the Minifter, who is now prefent, declares his entire concurrence.

Draft of a treaty propofed between the Company and Maha Raja Leukinda Bahadre.

Articles of agreement, made and concluded at Fort William, in Bengal, between the honourable the Governor-General and Council for the affairs of the Honourable Englifh Eaft India Company on the one part, and Maha Raja Leukinda Bahadre, Rana of Gohud, for himfelf and his fucceffors on the other part *.

Article 1ft. Perpetual friendfhip fhall take place between the Englifh Company and Maha Raga Leukindar

* The remarks made in the preceding articles are fufficient for thefe; with this only difference, that the alterations in this are powerfully in favour of the Rana, and againft the Company.

dar Bahadre and their fucceffors, and an alliance be
eftablifhed between them for the profecution of the
objects herein after mentioned.

2d. Whenever a war fhall actually take place between the contracting parties and the Marattas, if
Maha Raga Leukindar Bahadre fhall require the affiftance of an Englifh force from the Company for the
defence of his countries or for the acquifition of territory, fuch a force, proportioned to the exigency
of the fervice fhall be immediately fent, on his requifition made in writing to the commanding officer of
the neareft ftation of the Company's troops, and fhall
remain with him as long as he fhall require it, and return when he fhall difmifs it, the expences thereof
fhall be defrayed by the Maha Raja at the fixed
monthly rate of twenty thoufand Muchle dar rupees of
the currency of Benares, or any other fpecies of rupees
of the fame intrinfic amount for each battalion of fea-
poys on its prefent eftablifhment, with its proportion
of artillery; the payment to commence on the day
when the faid force fhall pafs the borders of the
Company's dominions, or the dominions of the Nabob
of Oude, and ceafe on the period ftipulated for the
return to either; four cofs being allowed for each day's
march.

3d. This force fhall be employed for the defence of
the Maha Raja's dominions againft all foreign or domeftic enemies, and for the enlargement of his dominions, by conqueft on the Marattas.

4th. Whatever countries fhall be acquired from the
Marattas in purfuance of this treaty by the troops of the
Company, or of the Maha Raja, feparately or in conjunction, whether by war or treaty, except the fifty-fix
mahls which conftitute the Maha Raja's jaghire, and

L   which

which are not now in the poffeffion of the Marattas, fhall be fhared in the following proportions, viz. nine annas to the Company, and feven annas to the Maha, Raja. The mean amount of the grofs revenue of the whole fhall be afcertained by ameens chofen by each party, on the collections made in the ten preceding years, and the amount of the Company's fhare, as determined by the faid ameens after deducting the charges of collection, which are cuftomary in fuch countries, fhall be: fixed and paid by the Maha Raja, as a perpetual tribute to the company; and the lands and forts fhall be ceded to the Maha Raja.

5th. In cafe it fhall be judged advifable to employ the combined forces of the company and the Maha Raja in any hoftile operations againft the Marattas, beyond the borders of the Maha Raja's dominions, on requifition made to him in writing from this government, he fhall furnifh ten thoufand horfe for fuch fervice, and each fhall bear his own feparate expence, and if upon the return of the Englifh forces, towards their own borders, the Maha Raja fhall have occafion for their fervices, and fhall make a requifition to retain them, from the inftant of fuch requifition he fhall pay their charge in the fame manner as ftipulated in the fecond article. But it fhall not be required of the Maha Raja, nor be in the power of this government, to detach or employ his troops beyond the borders of Gegur and Indoor, without fpecial confent.

6th. When the Englifh forces are employed for the defence of the Maha Raja's country, or for the acquifition of territory, the fervice to be performed fhall be prefcribed by himfelf, but the mode of executing it fhall be left to the decifion of the commanding officer of the Englifh troops.

7th.

7th. Whenever the combined troops of the company and the Maha Raja, fhall be employed in any remote operations, the commanding officer of the Englifh forces, fhall confult the Raja upon all fervices to be performed, but the ultimate decifion, in cafe of a difference of opinion, and the mode of conducting fuch fervices, fhall be left entirely to the commanding officer of the Englifh forces, with a refervation of the Maha Raja's compleat authority over his troops.

8th. Whenever peace fhall be concluded between the company and the Maratta ftate, the Maha Raja, fhall be included as a party in the treaty which fhall be made for that purpofe, and his prefent poffeffions, together with the fort of Gowallier, which of old belonged to the family of the Maha Raja, if it fhall be then in his poffeffion, and fuch countries as he fhall have acquired in the courfe of war, and which it fhall then be ftipulated to leave in his hands, fhall be guaranteed to him by fuch treaty.

9th. No Englifh factory fhall be eftablifhed in the dominions of the Maha Raja; no perfon of any denomination fhall be fent into his dominions on the part of the Englifh company, or with the licence of the governor general and council without his previous confent, neither fhall his ryots be preffed for any military fervice, nor any authority exercifed over them but his own.

Signed, fealed, and concluded at Fort William, this   day of   in the year of our Lord one thoufand feven hundred and feventy-nine, or the   day of

Mr. Wheler delivers in the following minute prepared in confequence of the governor general's former propofitions,

L 2

pofitions, which he thinks equally applicable to the prefent.

Mr. *Wheler*. I feel myfelf a great deal at a lofs. in giving my opinion on the fubject of the treaty propofed by the governor general with the Rana of Gohud, as I think a matter of fo much importance fhould not have been introduced without being accompanied with necef-fary information to enable the members of the board to judge of its expediency.

The Rana of Gohud, is, I believe, almoft a new name on our records. I am intirely unacquainted with the fituation even of his capital, except by confulting the map, the extent of his territory, his revenue, the force he is able to bring into the field, and his perfonal character, are points in which I am equally uninformed, nor do I believe any Englifhman, whofe authority can be depended upon, has ever been within the territories of Gohud, to afcertain them; yet thefe are points, on which the board ought to have the moft accurate infor-mation, before they proceed to decide on the propofed treaty; otherwife they may engage in a war with the Marattas, either to fupport, or make conqueft for a man who has neither means or capacity to enable him to bear any proportion in the rifque or charges which may attend fuch a war.

Uninformed, therefore, as I am, I can only give my opinion on the general principle of the propofed alliance; which is, that having for its object, war, conqueft, and increafe of territory, I conceive it to be contrary *to the true intereft of the Company and Britifh nation*, and to the fundamental policy of the former, and, in fact, changes the condition of the company here, from a commercial to a military ftate, that it is likewife in direct oppofition to all our inftructions, and peculiarly inexpedient at this time, when our treafury is exhaufted, thefe provinces

vinces drained of their specie, when the nation is engaged in a dangerous war in Europe, and the Company is threatened with a general combination of the Indian powers against all their settlements.

How, under such circumstances, the condition of the company is to be mended by hiring out their troops, and making conquest for a petty Raja, situated at so great a distance from their frontier, does not in anywise occur to me. I rather think that such alliance, and the measures proposed in consequence, are calculated to draw the neighbouring Marattas upon us, to expose our extensive and unguarded frontier to waste and ravage, and to involve the Company still more in danger and expence, without any adequate proposed advantage.

I am therefore against the treaty.

Mr. Francis delivered in the following minute upon this subject.

Mr. *Francis*, The Rana of Gohud is a prince with whom the Company have hitherto had no connection, and whose name, I believe, is unknown to them: I myself, I confess, have no other information concerning him, than what I have been able to collect within these few days. I see, by Major Rennell's map, that his capital is situated in latitude 26 deg. 20 min. long. west of Calcutta, 9 deg. 20 min. Gwallier, the place of which he wants to get possession, is a strong fortress in the hills, about eighty miles distant from Etawa, on the other side of the Jumna. From some officers who have been in that part of the country, I understand that the Rana is very poor, that his country is wild, rocky, and uncultivated; and that his army is little better than a rabble, ill armed and cloathed, and without regular pay or discipline. The governor-general's motion gives us no information on any of these points: -yet in the

con-

consideration of a question of such importance, as an immediate alliance, offensive and defensive, to be followed by a *future guarantee of future acquisitions*, it seems essential to us to know what are the strength and resources of the prince with whom we are going to engage; the situation and extent of his country, together with the circumstances and disposition of the powers who border upon it, and in whose differences with him, whatever there may be, we shall probably become parties, in consequence of our present engagements. Whether the conquest of Gwallier, is the Rana's sole and real object, *or whether another expedition into Bunalecund*, may not be in fact the consequence of our sending troops to act with him, is in my judgment very uncertain. Colonel Leslie set out under instructions, first to proceed to Bombay, and afterwards to Berar. Instead of doing either, he marched into Bundlecund, took possession of the capital, and remained there very quietly till he died. I think it not at all unlikely, that the officer who may command this expedition now projected, will follow the example of his immediate predecessor. There is nothing to be gained in the country of Gohud, or its neighbourhood, whereas the diamond country offers every temptation. It is the high road to fortune, and therefore the most likely to be pursued. Having no authentic information before me, on the state and condition of the Rana of Gohud, I must draw my conclusion from the best I have been able to obtain. Of course, they cannot be in favour of an alliance with a person so circumstanced as I believe the Rana of Gohud to be. At the same time I have no difficulty in declaring, that if all the facts were reversed, it would not incline me to assent to the measure. The event of these treaties in which we have hitherto engaged, or attempted to engage, does not furnish me with any encouragement to enter into new ones, formed on the same principles, or to follow that line of policy. I deem it unwise and dangerous

gerous in every fenfe. It is inconfiftent with the welfare
of Bengal to employ our forces in diftant fchemes of conqueft, whether for ourfelves or others. It is inconfiftent
with the fafety of Bengal to fend our troops acrofs the
Jumna, and much more to bind ourfelves to let them
remain there at the direction of any of the country powers. The diftance is too great, and the ftrength of the
Rana of Gohud too inconfiderable, to fuffer me to fup-
pofe it poffible, that the impreffions of any efforts of *his*,
or of ours in conjunction with him, can be felt on the
Malabar coaft, or create a diverfion that can be of the
fmalleft fervice to Brigadier-General Goddard.

But this, in my judgment, is not the moft material
confideration : the extent of our prefent frontier, to
fpeak moderately, and without the hazard of exaggera-
tion, is full as great as we are able to defend ; and if it
were not fo, a fyftem of invafion and conqueft is equally
unnatural, to the condition of the Eaft India company
as a mercantile body, and to that of the territory we pof-
fefs in India.

What fort of conclufions muft arife in the minds of
men at home, who are capable of judging of fuch queftions, when they fee that with all our prefent immenfe
poffeffions, and with all the revenues which we ought
to derive from them, it is neceffary to their fecurity that
we fhould endeavour to enlarge them. On the fame
principle, and from the fame caufes on which fuch meafures are deemed neceffary now, the future neceffity of
them muft increafe with every new acquifition. We
muft continue to conquer, as long as we continue to ac-
quire.

They who think fuch a fyftem of policy effential to
the fafety of the Company's actual poffeffions, muft admit, that our fituation in India is not only very preca-,
rious,

rious, but incapable of being fixed, once for all, upon a limited and folid foundation: but I am far from admitting that our eftablifhment here is of that nature, or that the meafures in queftion have any tendency to ftrengthen or fecure it. —— Mr. Wheler's minute to which I entirely fubfcribe, has anticipated a great deal of what I intended to have faid. I fhall therefore only add, that the fyftem of which this meafure makes a part, counteracts the fundamental principles of the Company's policy, and cannot be purfued without direct difobedience to their pofitive and repeated orders and inftructions to this government, nor without overfetting a principle laid down by the governor-general himfelf, and in which I entirely concnr, that " Notwithftanding " the fuperiority of the Britifh force in India, its general " line of action muft be purely defenfive."

" The terms of the propofed treaty are liable to many difficulties and objections. I fhall only mention one. Guarantees between princes and ftates are ufually, I believe, always reciprocal. There is a manifeft reafon, I confefs, for not calling upon the Rana of Gohud to guarrantee, as regularly as he ought to do, the poffeffion of future acquifitions to this government; but it is fuch a reafon as reduces the Rana very low, and ought to deter us from entering into any alliance with him. It may involve us into the conftaut fupport of his quarrels with his neighbours; but it offers us no compenfation or affiftance in return, fuppofing the Company's poffef- in any other part of India were invaded, nor is is it in his power to afford it.

Whether this be a juft obfervation or not, I need not infift upon it, becaufe my oppofition to the propofed treaty, is founded on principles which do not oblige me to canvafs the particular advantage, or difadvantage of every fpecific article contained in it. On that general ground

ground of argument, which Mr. Wheler has taken, and
to which I have only added a little, without improving
it. I entirely difapprove of the propofition, and proteſt
againſt it.

Mr. *Barwell.* The general objeɛt of the treaty appears to me pointed to the prefent circumſtances of our
government, and that of the Marattas. It ſtrikes me to
be well calculated to give ſtrength, to both the offenſive
means we hold within ourſelves, as to weaken thoſe of
our immediate enemies the Marattas. In a ſtate of war
with that power, every enemy that is raiſed up to their
ſtate, is an advantage to our own.——Plans of conqueſts,
acquiſition of territory, and a deſign to engage the forces
of the Company in diſtant expeditions, to which the ob-
jeɛtions of Mr. Wheler and Mr. Francis particularly
point, are not meditated by the preſent treaty. It is the
defence of theſe provinces and the diſtreſs of the common enemy, that appears to me to have led to this
treaty. If acquiſition of territory, or any advantage
ſhall ariſe from ſuch a policy, the Company and the nation will be benefited, without any of the riſques that
feem to be regarded with ſo much apprehenſion in the
foregoing minutes. I agree to the propoſed treaty.

Governor-General. I had no fufpicion that the members of this government could be ignorant of the confequence, much lefs of the exiſtence of the Rana of Gohud; it was therefore unneceſſary for me to have in-
ſtruɛted them on theſe points. *Nor was I forward to in-
troduce a meaſure of felf-apparent neceſſity, with arguments
which I know would be conteſted,* and the meaſure of courſe
oppoſed. We were upon the eve of a war with the
Maratta ſtate; a war which is no lefs the effeɛt
of the Company's decided orders, 'than of the
meaſures of their ſervants, to which this government
has given its fanɛtion. From General Goddard's ad-

M   vices

vices it may be almost positively concluded, that we are
actually in a state of war with them, *and possibly with
other powers combined* with them. Had this government
remained in total inaction, had no measure of this kind
been adopted, I should expect to be reproached with
suffering the Company to be drawn into a war, with
perhaps the first power in India, without any alliance to
'support it, or to obviate the predatory incursions of such
an enemy. I am now reproached with forming such an
alliance, and on grounds which will not apply to a state
of perfect peace and domestic security. Were the ac-
quisition of territory, or the increase of revenue the object,
the operations of the treaty would not be limited to the
seasons of war. If war has taken place, or shall take
place with the Maratta state, the treaty secures the support and assistance of a powerful Prince, whose dominions adjoin to our own frontier, and lie in one of
the principal roads through which the Marattas must
pass to invade us, and the objects proposed by the
alliance, are such as are most likely to weaken the Maratta state, by depriving it of its resources, and divi-
ding its attention. At the same time, the principal in
the treaty with us, is a man whose personal interests
and enmity to the Maratta state, we may depend on for
his faithful adherence to it. He succeeded to his present possessions by the death of his father, who lost his
life, and the fortess of Gwalier at the same time, in an
engagement with the Marattas, with whom the son has
ever since been in a state of warfare. It is notorious,
and will be probably known to many well-informed
persons at home, that the Marattas have made various
attempts to reduce the present Rana with numerous armies conducted by their most eminent leaders, and
once by Raganaut Row in person; and have been as
often repulsed with discredit to their government, and
honour to the Rana. *That he was the protector of two of
the most important and obnoxious characters in Hindostan.*

Gauzi,

Gauzi, Ollien Cawn, and Coffim Ali Cawn, are facts so notorious, that I cannot yet suppose any member of this board to be ignorant of them; and there are not only presumptive. but very strong proofs of the power of the man, whose state could prove an asylum to such fugitives. His personal abilities are equally known. They are universally acknowledged, and proved by his actions.

I have said that the object of the treaty, and the operations dependent on it, are restricted to a state of war with the Marattas. A war, in which with respect to the immediate commencement of it, independent of former causes, *they must be the aggressors, by rejecting the offers of peace which we have made to them.*—If after all, my supposition should not be realized by the event, but a peace ensue, the treaty becomes in itself null, being reduced to the simple tie of friendship, which alters nothing of the relative state in which we are at present with the Rana ; and all the consequences which Mr. Francis concludes that it will entail upon us, which suppose a war with the Marattas, are certainly more likely to happen from such a war, if we have no support, than with a provision to avert them.—I have had such frequent occasion to complain of the unfair manner in which Mr. Francis quotes my words and opinions, that I shall make no other reply to his assertion of the contradiction of the present measure to my own principles, than that the expression which he has quoted appertains to a different occasion, and a different object, and bears no more relation to the present subject, than the dispatch of treasure to Bombay or Surat.

Mr. *Francis.* Neither Mr. Wheeler nor I, have professed to be ignorant of the existence of the Rana of Gohud ; but when a treaty offensive and defensive is

proposed to be concluded with him, I presume it is not enough to know that he exists. I, for my own part, should have held myself indebted to the Governor-General, as I always am, for any information he might have thought proper to give me of the circumstances and situation of this Rajah. It is probable that I might have endeavoured to obtain it myself from other quarters, if at any period since my arrival in Bengal, I had thought it possible that an intimate connection of interests between the Company and him should ever have been proposed. When a similar treaty was in agitation with a much greater Prince, I mean Modajee Boosla, the Governor-General introduced the proposition with a very particular report of his situation, views, family, connections, resources, and interests. The lights which the Governor-General's last minute have furnished me, do not tend to establish a favourable opinion either of the Rana's character or strength. I do not wish to be connected with a man who is only known by the protection he afforded to persons so obnoxious to this government, and to India in general, as Cossim Ali Cawn, and Gauzi Odien Cawn; and as to the strength which enabled him to give them that protection, I believe it to be purely defensive. He is a hill Rajah. I conclude he has strong holds in the mountains, and that it is not easy to come at him. Admitting it to be true, that at this time, and to support a war, which it is said is the effect of the decided orders of the Company, alliances with some of the country powers might be useful and necessary. It does not follow that all and every alliance deserves that character. It is not at all unlikely, that we may find ourselves encumbered and embarrassed with the burthen of a useless ally. I mean to use the words applied by the Governor-General not long ago, to our connection with Ragoba, and I am sure I express the sense of them; an offensive union with Hyder Ally, or the Nizam, or even with the Raja
of

of Berar, if he could be feparated from his countrymen, might indeed on the principles of the prefent war be of importance to its fuccefs. The Rana of Gohud is too inconfiderable to be of weight in either fcale ; but if his ftrength were greater than it is, it would not neceffarily follow that we fhould gain any thing by uniting it to ours. Before fuch a junction can be effected, we muft crofs the Jumna, and relinquifh all the fecurity and other advantages which the intervention of that great barrier affords to all our poffeffions, and to thofe of our ally. By the faid act we divide our force, and make it difficult, if not impracticable, for the different parts of it fo feparated, to affift each other. Every operation we undertake on either fide of the river, fo far from adding to our ftrength, or diftreffing the enemy, is only laying ourfelves open to wounds in a quarter where, if we ftaid within our barrier, we might be invulnerable. We relinquifh a fituation of fuperior ftrength, to meet an enemy, if we do meet him on equal terms. I fhall trouble the board but with one word more. The Governor-General, it is true, has often complained of unfair quotations ; and this complaint I am informed, has been echoed in England, but I do not admit that it has ever been made with reafon ; let an inftance of any moment be pointed out, and I am ready to join iffue upon it.

Governor-General. . I have never made the complaint againft Mr. Francis of an unfair quotation, but I have pointed out the inftances and proved them to be unfair. The prefent inftance is before us. I do remember that when we were firft informed of a war between Great-Britain and France, I faid that our part of the war muft be purely defenfive, becaufe they had all to gain, and we to lofe. I do not know that thefe were the words, but I am fure that this was the fubftance and fenfe of the maxim which is now quoted as a contradiction

tradiction to the propofal which I make of withftanding a predatory enemy, already in poffeffion of a great part of Hindoftan, by diftant and offenfive operations. For the reft of Mr. Francis's minute, I do not think it neceffary to reply to it, having, I think, in all our contefts allowed him the laft argument; and I think the fubject was fufficiently difcuffed in the preceding minutes.

Mr. *Francis.* I admit that the maxim which I have attributed to the Governor-General, was introduced on the occafion he mentions; I neverthelefs underftood it to be a general one, at leaft, it certainly could not be confined to the cafe of a war with France, fince at the fame point of time we ftrongly recommended, and by our affiftance promoted the fiege of Pondicherry.

Governor-General. Let it be added, that I at the fame time propofed a meafure, which from its tendency led to the poffibility at leaft of an offenfive war with the Marattas. And this propofition was made in the fame minute 'in which the maxim now attributed to me was introduced; and I will venture to fay, will not be underftood from thefe minutes; neither from thofe of Mr. Francis and my own.

Agreed to the amended draught of the treaty.

Ordered to be engroffed fair, and executed.

Extract Secret Department Confultations,

6th December, 1779.

The following minute from the Governor-General was fent in on Saturday laft; and agreeable to his direction was circulated to the members of the the board.

Governor

Governor-General. Having in confequence of the treaty paffed the board for an 'alliance with the Rana of Gohud, required his Vakeel to produce the powers with which he was invefted for executing it on the part of his mafter, he delivered me a paper which I fhall lay before the board at their next meeting, containing fimply the Rajah's public feal, and which with his letters, declaring the Vakeel to be deputed for the purpofe of concluding fuch a treaty, are deemed fufficient and ample authority according to the form and ufage of Hindoftan; but as the Rana has not fet his name to the paper, and with us the fignatures of the contracting parties are held indifpenfible to the validity of all the public engagements, I informed the Vakeel of this defect in his powers. He requefted that they might, with the addition of his own feal and fignature, be admitted for the prefent execution of the treaty, and to remove all doubt, and authenticate it according to our forms, he made me a propofal, which I now lay before the board, under his hand and feal, for fending a perfon on the part of this government to witnefs the Rana's final execution of it, and exchange the ratification; and I recommend it for their approbation.

(Signed)　　WARREN HASTINGS.

Arzee from Muzhar Ally, Vakeel of the Rana of Gohud.

" As I underftand from what you faid, that the cuftoms of your country require contracting parties fhould fign their names to the treaty, to give it credit and validity, I am therefore hopeful, and make it my requeft, that fince the Rajah in his letters to you, has affured you of the validity of my powers, you will for the prefent accept of a furd with my fignature, and the feal of the Maha Rajah; and that a gentleman of truft

may

may be fent to the Maha Rajah, that all the points which have been fettled here, may be finally concluded there, in the prefence of fuch gentleman; and that in like manner as I have reprefented many things on the part of the Maha Rajah, fuch gentleman may obtain fatisfaction in all matters, and fee the Maha Rajah fet his fignature to the treaty. This will be highly pleafing to the Maha Rajah, and gain me credit with you."

The following opinions were returned to the above minute and Arzee.

" I agree to the propofitions.

(Signed)   R. BARWELL."

Mr. *Francis.* If the Vakeel be not invefted with fufficient powers to execute the treaty on the part of his conftituent, we ought not to have proceeded with him fo far as we have done. The extent of his powers fhould regularly have been afcertained in the firft inftance. For my own part, I am perfectly fatisfied with the Rajah's feal, and the contents of his letters. It is not likely that he fhould refufe to ratify a treaty by which he is entitled to, and impowered to require the affiftance of our forces, *for the defence of his country, or for the acquifition of territory,* without any other limitation or defcription of the amount of fuch force to be fent, *immediately on his requifition,* except that it fhall be proportioned to the exigency of the fervice : of which the Rana is to be the judge. The deputing a gentleman, on purpofe to Gohud, to fee the treaty ratified. is, in my opinion, a very ufelefs, and I am fure it will be a very expenfive meafure. I am therefore entirely againft it. I do not even know that the Rana's fignature is wanted.

wanted. The public feal on both fides is the true au-
thentication of their public acts refpectively.

(Signed)   P. FRANCIS.

(Agreed to the above,)   E. WHEELER.

Refolved, That a perfon on the part of this government be deputed to the Rana of Gohud, *for the purpofe
of feeing the treaty executed by the Rana, and for the changing
the ratification.*

The Governor-General now produces to the board
the power and treaty above recorded, under the feal
of the Rana of Gohud.

Vide, the Book of Perfian Correfpondence under
date.

The Governor-General thinks it incumbent on him
to lay before the board the following paper of intelligence, which was inclofed in a letter to him from the
Commander in Chief.

Extract of a letter from Futty-gur, 20th Nov. 1779.

" I have likewife juft now received from Gohud,
the difagreeable news of the Marattas having made
themfelves mafters of the fort Arhaund, (which I had
the honour to inform you fome time ago was invefted)
and put the garrifon to the fword. The fame account
informs me, that they are preparing to attack another
fort, and that the Rajah is by no means in a condition
to oppofe them; his troops being not only inferior in
point of number to the enemy, but alfo difpirited and
ready to mutiny, on account of the long arrears due to
them, which he is at prefent unable to pay. In this
fituation of his affairs, the fpeedy conqueft of his whole

N   country

country muſt be the conſequence of the enemy's purſuing their advantage with that briſkneſs which the defence-leſs ſtate of it ſeems to invite."

Governor General. Having communicated this intelligence to Meer Muzzur Ally, the Rajah's Miniſter, he informed me, that he had received no letter from his maſter ſince his arrival, and therefore concluded that the danger ſtated as impending on his country from the Maratta invaſion, had been much exaggerated ; but thought it probable that the port of Arhaund, mentioned in the intelligence, had been taken by the Marattas ; that it was ſituated in the ſouthern extremity of his dominions, and not capable of much reſiſtance. There can be no doubt that a Maratta force has entered the territories of the Rana of Gohud, though of itſelf not likely to be productive of any material conſequence. It appears to me to be part of a plan, which I was lately informed by a channel which I have hitherto experienced to be of good authority, had been conſulted by the ruling adminiſtration of Poona, for the general conduct of the war againſt the Company, namely, that Nana Furneſe and Hurry Punt Furkia were to conduct the war againſt General Goddard ; and that Madagee Scindia and Tuccajee Holkar were to unite their forces, and proceed immediately againſt the Rana of Gohud, to reduce his country, and afterwards enter the Douab, and the dominions of the Nabob of Oude, or into the countries dependent on Bengal; as the circumſtances of the times ſhould direct them probably to either. I have ſince heard that this plan has been changed, and that all the chiefs above mentioned had united their forces, and were preparing to march directly againſt General Goddard. It appears however, equally neceſ-ſary to guard againſt any attempts which may have been projected againſt the Rana of Gohud, and to ſtrengthen

his

his hands, to enable him the better to act in concert
with us, if that defign, from whatever caufe, fhall have
been fufpended. I therefore move, that a copy of the
treaty which it has been agreed to conclude with the
Rana of Gohud, be immediately tranfmitted to the
Commander in Chief, with inftructions to comply with
any immediate requifition which the Rana may make
for a detachment of our forces, proportioned to the
exigency of the fervice required by it, of which he will
of courfe be the judge.

Mr. Wheeler. I am againft the motion.

Mr. Francis. If the Board were difpofed to make a
right ufe of the intelligence contained in the preceding
letter, I fhould have thought it a fortunate circum-
ftance, that we had received it before any thing had
been finally concluded with the Rana's Vakeel. The
Rana of Gohud's fituation appears, by this letter, to
be confiderably worfe than it was reprefented to me.
One of his forts was taken; the Marattas were preparing to take another, and the fpeedy conqueft of the
whole country was likely to be the confequence. If
this be the cafe, we are going to execute a treaty with
a Prince, who may have neither army nor any dominions left. His army is difpirited, and ready to mutiny
for want of pay, which he is unable to give them. If
he cannot pay his own troops, how will it be poffible for
him to difcharge the fubfidy which he engaged to pay
for ours? Inftead of enlarging his territories by conqueft, which is the profeffed object of the treaty, our
firft labour will be to recover for him, what he has
already loft; and this muft be attempted by marching
part of our army to a confiderable diftance on the other
fide of the Jumna. I do not confider the prefent invafion of his country by the Marattas, as belonging to,

or

or the effect of any particular plan of operations against the Company. He is at constant enmity with the Marattas, and I look upon this attack as nothing more than the continuance of former hostilities against him. At all events we shall only distress ourselves, and abandon the protection of our frontier, by engaging in his defence. I am, therefore, against the motion.

Mr. *Barwell.* I agree to the motion. I cannot adopt the opinion, that to allow the Marattas to conquer a country, so near our frontier, and extend their possessions quite up to it, will be attended with any of those advantages which have been supposed as the probable result of our not opposing their progress. The intelligence that has been lain before the Board, rather determines me to engage our government in the support of the Rana of Gohud, than to leave the country an easy conquest to the only enemy from whom we have reason to apprehend any mischief.

Agreed to the Governor-General's motion. And ordered that a copy of the treaty with the Rana of Gohud, be immediately transmitted to the Commander in Chief.

Secret Department Consultation, Eec. 13, 1779.

The *Governor-General* proposes that Captain Palmer be permitted to draw the same allowances during his deputation to Gohud, as were assigned to Mr. Elliot, on his deputation to Berar. And that Mr. Tho. Short be appointed assistant to Captain Palmer, with the same allowances as were granted to Mr. Farquhar, assistant to Mr. Elliot.

Mr. *Wheeler.* I have not yet considered the business which

which Captain Palmer is going to undertake, in the light, or of the fame importance with that which was entrusted to the charge of Mr. Elliot. At this diſtance of time, I do not properly recollect, whether the allowances given to that gentlemen, were not objected to by me. However, I do not mean to revert to a former opinion, upon a ſubject ſo perſonal as the preſent; though I would wiſh the allowances had been ſuch on this occaſion, as I ſhould have judged ſafe to have acceded to, which, as they are now ſtated, I muſt beg leave to decline.

Mr. *Francis.* Mr. Elliott's allowances amounted to 3318 cur. rup. per month, thoſe of his aſſiſtants to 555, in all 3873. I think they are much too high for the preſent occaſion ; and as Captain Palmer is only deputed to ſee the treaty with the Rana executed, he cannot have any uſe or employment for an aſſiſtant.

Mr. *Barwell.* I think the allowances for Mr. Elliot, were regulated by thoſe allotted to Colonel Upton, on his embaſſy to Poona; and however large they may have appeared to the Court of Directors, I have reaſon to think that neither Colonel Upton nor Mr. Elliott were enabled to make any conſiderable ſaving from their allowances. The circumſtances in which Captain Palmer is placed, is nearly the ſame, and the appearance he muſt make, muſt be regulated upon the ſame principle. The difference of rank between Colonel Upton and Captain Palmer can be no rule to direct the judgment, on this occaſion. He is the ſervant of Government, in the ſame line as Colonel Upton was, and he muſt ſupport the ſame character. I therefore aſſent to the motion.

Agreed. That Captain Palmer be permitted to draw
the

the fame allowances as Mr. Elliott, viz. Lieutenant-
Colonel's pay, and double batta 1488 fonat rupees
per month, fixed falary 1000; and contingencies, including mounchies, fervants, &c. 500. That Mr.
Short, as affiftant to Catain Palmer, be allowed the fame
as Mr. Farquar, viz. pay and batta of a Captain, 512
fonat rupees per month.

F I N I S.

www.ingramcontent.com/pod-product-compliance
Lightning Source LLC
Chambersburg PA
CBHW030552270326
41927CB00008B/1610